Ipso Factos:

C000094092

Ipso Factos: EU Law

Emma Barry BL

Bloomsbury Professional

Published by
Bloomsbury Professional
Maxwelton House
41–43 Boltro Road
Haywards Heath
West Sussex
RH16 1BJ

Bloomsbury Professional
The Fitzwilliam Business Centre
26 Upper Pembroke Street
Dublin 2

ISBN 978 1 78043 679 1

© Bloomsbury Professional Limited 2014
Bloomsbury Professional, an imprint of Bloomsbury Publishing Plc

All rights reserved. No part of this publication may be reproduced in any material form (including photocopying or storing it in any medium by electronic means and whether or not transiently or incidentally to some other use of this publication) without the written permission of the copyright owner except in accordance with the provisions of the Copyright, Designs and Patents Act 1988 or under the terms of a licence issued by the Copyright Licensing Agency Ltd., Saffron House, 6–10 Kirby Street, London, EC1N 8TS, England. Applications for the copyright owner's written permission to reproduce any part of this publication should be addressed to the publisher.

Warning: The doing of an unauthorised act in relation to a copyright work may result in both a civil claim for damages and criminal prosecution.

This work is intended to be a general guide and cannot be a substitute for professional advice. Neither the authors nor the publisher accept any responsibility for loss occasioned to any person acting or refraining from acting as a result of material contained in this publication.

While every care has been taken to ensure the accuracy of this work, no responsibility for loss or damage occasioned to any person acting or refraining from action as a result of any statement in it can be accepted by the authors, editors or publishers.

British Library Cataloguing-in-Publication Data
A catalogue record for this book is available from the British Library

Typeset by Marie Armah-Kwantreng, Dublin, Ireland
Printed in Great Britain by
Printed in Great Britain by CPI Group (UK) Ltd, Croydon, CR0 4YY

CONTENTS

Contents

Contents

TABLE OF CASES

G

H

I

J

K

N

O

P

R

TABLE OF STATUTES

TABLE OF EU LEGISLATION

TABLE OF INTERNATIONAL AGREEMENTS

TABLE OF CONSTITUTIONS

Chapter 1

The History of the European Union

THE SCHUMAN DECLARATION 1950

[1.01] In the first half of the twentieth century, Europe was devastated by two World Wars. Following these two wars, the people of Europe wanted continued peace and in order to achieve this goal political and economic cooperation was seen as the way forward.

The first steps toward political and economic cooperation began with the Schuman Declaration in 1950. The Schuman Declaration related to the production of coal and steel in France and Germany, the aim of which was to have the coal and steel industries controlled by a High Authority to operate at a supranational level. Supranational control meant that the High Authority would operate above and independently of the French and German governments. By preventing states from maintaining exclusive control over the production of coal and steel, which are the raw materials of war, it was hoped that the possibility of war would be reduced.

THE EUROPEAN COAL AND STEEL COMMUNITY TREATY 1951

[1.02] The Schuman Declaration was implemented by a Treaty signed in Paris in 1951 which established the European Coal and Steel Community (ECSC). This Treaty was signed by France, Germany, Italy, Belgium, the Netherlands and Luxembourg.

The ECSC Treaty created a common market in coal and steel and provided for the creation of four supranational institutions to facilitate the running of this common market. The executive institution was the High Authority which had decision-making power and was responsible for implementing the aims of the Treaty. The second institution was an Assembly which had an advisory role and consisted of delegates from the national parliaments. The third institution was a Council which had some decision-making powers in addition to a consultative role and comprises one representative of each of the national governments. The fourth institution was a Court of Justice made up of nine judges.

The ECSC was a significant development in that it represented the first steps towards European integration. The ECSC existed for 50 years and expired in 2002.

THE EEC AND EURATOM TREATIES 1957

[1.03] Two treaties were signed in Rome in 1957, the European Atomic Energy Community Treaty (EURATOM) and the European Economic Community Treaty (EEC). These treaties were signed by the same six countries that had signed the ECSC Treaty.

The EURATOM Treaty regulated nuclear power and it was hoped that cooperation in the development of atomic energy would help keep peace in post-war Europe.

The EEC Treaty advanced economic integration beyond coal and steel and created a common market. The common market allowed for free movement of goods between the six Member States and a common customs tariff on all goods entering the common market. In addition, the EEC Treaty introduced common agricultural policies and common transport policies.

An institutional framework for the EEC was also established consisting of, the Assembly (now the European Parliament), the Council, the Commission and the Court of Justice. This institutional framework still exists although the respective institutions' powers and functions have changed over the years. In 1965, attempts were made to streamline the administration by means of the Merger Treaty. This treaty came into force in 1967 and it merged the institutions established by the ECSC, EURATOM and EEC Treaties. As a result, from 1967 there was one European Commission, one Council of Ministers and one Assembly (now the European Parliament).

SINGLE EUROPEAN ACT 1986

[1.04] The main aim of the Single European Act (SEA) was the completion of the internal market by the removal of the remaining barriers to trade. A timeframe was set for this to be achieved over a period expiring on 31 December 1992.

The SEA officially changed the name of the European Assembly to the European Parliament and formal recognition was also given to the European Council. A new cooperation procedure was introduced whereby qualified majority voting for the Council of Ministers was established and the powers of the European Parliament were increased.

The areas of Community competence were extended to include health and safety at work, economic and social cohesion, research and development, and environmental protection.

Students should note that the European Council and the Council of Ministers are two separate entities. The Council of Ministers consists of ministers from the Member States. The European Council comprises the heads of state of the Member States. We will look at the different institutions in more detail later in the course.

THE TREATY ON EUROPEAN UNION 1992

[1.05] The Treaty on European Union (TEU) was signed in Maastricht in February 1992. This treaty encountered a difficult ratification process in Germany and Denmark and finally came into force on the 1 November 1993. The TEU was a far-reaching treaty; it introduced extensive changes and created the European Union (EU).

As a result of the TEU, the word 'economic' was removed from the EEC Treaty. The EEC Treaty was renamed the EC Treaty in order to show that the goals of the Community went beyond the original economic goals.

The TEU created a three-pillar structure in respect of the governance of the EU. The first pillar was the Community Pillar comprising the

3

ECSC, EURATOM and EC. The second pillar consisted of a Common Foreign and Security Policy. The third pillar addressed Justice and Home Affairs. The EU was an umbrella term for all EU activity carried out under the three pillars.

The EU had supranational power in relation to the Community Pillar. This meant that the Institutions of the EU had the power to make decisions on matters relating to this pillar independently of the Member States. By contrast, intergovernmental negotiations between the Member States were required in relation to the second and third pillars. The requirement of intergovernmental negotiations meant that decisions were made by the Member States acting as independent sovereign states.

TREATY OF AMSTERDAM 1997

[1.06] The Treaty of Amsterdam was created in order to address the restructuring of the Community institutions in preparation for enlargement. However, the institutional restructuring was deferred and was addressed later by the Treaty of Nice.

The Treaty of Amsterdam reformed the Community legislative process and made changes across the three-pillar structure of the EU. The purpose of these changes was to create a more integrated EU legal order.

Immigration policy was incorporated into the Community Pillar by the insertion of a new title into the EC Treaty entitled 'Visas, Asylum and Immigration'. A further change was made to the third pillar by renaming 'Justice and Home Affairs' as 'Police and Judicial Co-operation in Criminal Matters'. These changes also meant that the intergovernmental role in the third pillar was being reduced. The primary effect of the changes was that immigration policy was subject to supranational control and that legislation in this area was subject to judicial review by the Court of Justice.

The Treaty of Amsterdam came into effect on the 1 May 1999.

THE TREATY OF NICE 2001

[1.07] The Treaty of Nice began the preparations for enlargement which had not been addressed by the Treaty of Amsterdam. The Treaty of Nice was signed in 2001; however, it did not enter into force until 1 February 2003. The Treaty was initially rejected by the Irish citizens in a 2001 referendum, though it was subsequently accepted in a second referendum in 2002.

The Treaty of Nice facilitated the accession of 10 new Member States through institutional restructuring. This restructuring related to qualified majority voting, the co-decision procedure and the composition of the European institutions.

ENLARGEMENT

[1.08] The original six members of the Community were France, Germany, Italy, Belgium, the Netherlands and Luxembourg. The membership remained unchanged until the Republic of Ireland, the UK and Denmark joined in 1973. In 1981, Greece became a member and Spain and Portugal joined in 1986. In 1990, as a result of the reunification of Germany, East Germany was assimilated. Austria, Finland and Sweden joined the EU in 1995 and, in 2004, Cyprus, the Czech Republic, Estonia, Hungary, Latvia, Lithuania, Malta, Poland, Slovakia and Slovenia became members. In 2007, Romania and Bulgaria joined and in 2013, Croatia joined, bringing the total number of Member States to 28.

THE CONSTITUTIONAL TREATY

[1.09] Following the Nice Treaty, a Declaration on the Future of the European Union was adopted which called for a deeper and wider debate about the future of the EU. In 2001, the Laeken European Council began a process whereby all the Member States and the proposed Accession States discussed the future of the EU.

After much deliberation and amendment, the Treaty Establishing a Constitution for Europe was signed in Rome in 2004. However, the ratification process encountered a great deal of criticism and opposition. In 2005, the Treaty was rejected in referenda held in France and the Netherlands, following which the ratification process was abandoned.

THE TREATY OF LISBON 2007

[1.10] In June 2007, following a two-year period of reflection, an Intergovernmental Conference (IGC) began work on drafting a Reform Treaty. The Treaty of Lisbon (the Reform Treaty) was signed on the 13 December 2007. When the Treaty was rejected by the Irish citizens in a referendum held in June 2008, the future of the Treaty remained uncertain. However, the Irish citizens accepted the Treaty in a second referendum held in October 2009 and the Treaty of Lisbon entered into force on the 1 December 2009.

The main objective of the Lisbon Treaty is to make the EU more democratic and efficient. The Treaty amends the TEU and the EC Treaty; it does not replace them. The Treaty has renamed the EC Treaty so that it is now called The Treaty on the Functioning of the European Union (TFEU). All references to 'the Community' have now been replaced with 'the Union' and the TFEU and the amended TEU are the treaties upon which the Union is founded.

The Lisbon Treaty abolished the three-pillar structure which formerly existed. As a result, the majority of decisions will now be made at a European supranational level and not through intergovernmental negotiations. As a result of these changes, Ireland, Denmark and the UK have negotiated opt-outs in the area of freedom, security and justice.

Prior to the Treaty of Lisbon, under the three-pillar structure only the European Communities Pillar had its own legal personality. When the three-pillar structure was abolished by the Lisbon Treaty, it was replaced with a consolidated legal personality for the Union. The EU now has a legal personality, which means that it can become a member of international organisations and can enter into international agreements; it is expected that this will strengthen the Union's negotiating power on the world stage.

A new position has been created in the Union for a High Representative in the area of Foreign Affairs and Security Policy. The High Representative coordinates and carries out the Foreign Affairs and Security policy for the European Union. The High Representative's role is wide-ranging and includes the following;

- Participation in the development of and implementation of Common Foreign Policy and Security Policy as mandated by the Council;

- Responsibility for external relations and the coordination of the European Union's external action;

- Responsibility for Common Security and Defence Policy;

- The High Representative is one of the five Vice Presidents of the European Commission and presides over the Foreign Affairs Council.

A European External Action Service will assist the High Representative. The service is comprised of officials from the General Secretariat of the Council and the Commission and individuals seconded from national diplomatic services. The European External Action Service works in cooperation with the national diplomatic services in the Member States.

Charter of Fundamental Rights

[1.11] The Treaty of Lisbon introduced the Charter of Fundamental Rights of the European Union 2000 into European primary law. The European courts are able to apply and interpret the Charter of Fundamental Rights, which the Treaty of Lisbon recognises as having the same legal value as the Treaties. The Member States must respect the rights written in the Charter when they are implementing EU Law. However, Poland and the UK have negotiated opt-outs.

The Citizens' Initiative

[1.12] The Lisbon Treaty introduced the interesting concept of 'The Citizens' Initiative', which is a new form of public participation in the European Union. The Citizens' Initiative makes it possible for citizens to directly request that the Commission brings forward and considers an issue within EU competence. Citizens may make this request once one million signatures have been collected. The Commission is obliged to consider the request, but it is not obliged to act on it. It is hoped that the Citizens' Initiative will give citizens a stronger voice within the European Union.

The Lisbon Treaty gives effect to substantial institutional changes which will be considered in the next chapter, 'The Institutions of the European Union'.

Chapter 2

The Institutions

INTRODUCTION

[2.01] In 1957, the EEC Treaty established the institutions of the EEC consisting of, the Assembly (now the European Parliament), the Council, the Commission and the Court of Justice. This institutional framework still exists although the respective institutions' powers and functions have changed over the years.

The European Council (this institution is to be distinguished from the Council) and the European Central Bank are now full Union institutions following the coming into force of the Lisbon Treaty.

According to Art 13 TEU (ex Art 7 EC) the principal institutions of the EU are:

1. the European Parliament,
2. the European Council,
3. the Council,
4. the European Commission,
5. the Court of Justice of the European Union,
6. the European Central Bank,
7. the Court of Auditors.

THE EUROPEAN PARLIAMENT

[2.02] The seat of the European Parliament is in Strasbourg, France. However, certain sessions and committee meetings take place in Brussels.

The European Parliament is the only directly elected body of the European Union. There are currently 751 Members of the European Parliament. The MEPs are elected once every five years by the citizens from the 28 member states. The European Parliament elects its own President for a renewable term of two and a half years. The seats in Parliament are shared out proportionately to the population of each Member State. However, this method of allocation has been criticised as it is not strictly proportional to population size and there are difficulties with over-representation. For example, France has 74 seats whereas Spain has 54 seats.

Following Croatia's accession in 2013, a reshuffle of the seats was required in order to maintain representation for the newest Member State and this saw some countries losing seats. The requests for seats to be distributed in an objective, fair, transparent and durable manner is being taken into account and the European Parliament is attempting to put in place a revised seat allocation that represents balance for the 2019 elections.

Once an MEP is elected they sit according to their political affinity and not their nationality. There are currently seven political groups in the European Parliament;

- Group of the European People's Party (Christian Democrats)
- Group of the Progressive Alliance of Socialists and Democrats in the European Parliament.
- Group of the Alliance of Liberals and Democrats for Europe.
- Group of the Greens/European Free Alliance.
- European Conservatives and Reformists Group
- Confederal Group of the European United Left – Nordic Green Left
- Europe of Freedom and Democracy Group

There are rules relating to the number of MEPs. Following the Lisbon Treaty and according to Article 14 TEU the maximum number of MEPs, including the President, has been be raised to 751. There are now a minimum of six MEPs per Member State and no Member State has more than 96 MEPs.

Powers of the European Parliament

Legislative Powers

[2.03] The European Parliament's involvement in the legislative process was initiated by the Single European Act 1986 (SEA). Prior to this the Parliament's involvement was purely advisory and consultative.

The SEA introduced the cooperation procedure which attributed more power to the Parliament. The Maastricht Treaty (TEU) introduced the co-decision procedure which once again increased the Parliament's power in the legislative process. The Treaty of Amsterdam extended the co-decision procedure and the same weight was given to the Council and the Parliament on a number of legislative areas. The Treaty of Nice also increased the role of Parliament. The Lisbon Treaty further increased the Parliament's power by introducing the ordinary legislative procedure which gives the same weight to the Parliament and the Council on a broad range of areas such as immigration, energy, transport, environment and consumer protection. The majority of EU laws are now jointly adopted by the Parliament and the Council.

The legislative procedures of the European Union will be considered in detail later in **Ch 4**.

Additional Powers

[2.04] The Parliament and the Council both work together as the Union's budgetary authority. The budgetary authority prepares and adopts the budget each year.

The Parliament has a number of supervisory powers:

- Every EU citizen has the right to petition Parliament in order to seek a remedy for any problems arising in relation to European Union activity.

- An ombudsman has been appointed by Parliament to deal with complaints made by EU citizens against EU institutions and bodies.

- The Parliament has the power to set up a committee of inquiry in order to investigate the contravention or incorrect application of Community law by Member States.

- Parliament can apply to the Court of Justice for the annulment of an EU act and Parliament can bring an action against the Commission or the Council if they fail to fulfil their obligations.

- Parliament can approve or reject the Council's nomination for President of the Commission.

- Parliament has the power to censure the Commission. The Parliament can force the Commission to resign if the motion of the Parliament is carried by a two-thirds majority.

THE COUNCIL

[2.05] The Council of Ministers is commonly referred to as the Council. It should be noted that the European Council and the Council of Ministers are two separate entities. The role of the European Council will be outlined later in this chapter.

The seat of the Council of Ministers is in Brussels, Belgium and it consists of Ministers from the national governments of the Member States. The Council shares the legislative function with the Parliament and it carries out policy-making and co-ordination functions as laid down in the Treaties. The national ministers who attend the Council have the authority to vote and commit their governments. The Council represents the interests of the Member States.

The Council does not always consist of the same national ministers. The composition of the Council will vary according to the policy area under discussion. The policy areas are divided into what is called 'configurations' and the ministers from the Member States attend the configuration that they are responsible for.

Following the Lisbon Treaty there are now ten configurations:

1. General Affairs;

2. Foreign Affairs;

3. Economic and Financial Affairs;

4. Justice and Home Affairs;

5. Employment, Social Policy, Health and Consumer Affairs;

6. Competitiveness (internal market, industry, research and space);

7. Transport, Telecommunications and Energy;

8. Agriculture and Fisheries;

9. Environment;

10. Education, youth, culture and sport.

When the Council adopts a decision it does so as the Council and no reference is made to the configuration that made the decision.

Presidency

[2.06] The Presidency of the Council is held for six months by each Member State on a rotational basis.

Powers of the Council

[2.07] The Council is responsible for decision making and co-ordination in a number of areas:

- The Council passes laws and legislates jointly with the Parliament. The Council must give approval to the Commission's proposals before they can become law.

- The Council co-ordinates the Member States' economic policies.

- The Council implements EU common foreign and security policy.

- The Council concludes international agreements on behalf of the EU.

- The Council adopts measures in the area of police and judicial co-operation in criminal matters.

- The Council and the Parliament work together as the Union's budgetary authority.

Legislation

[2.08] The acts adopted by the Council take the form of regulations, directives, decisions, common actions, recommendations or opinions.

The Council also adopts conclusions, declarations and resolutions.

Voting

[2.09] All the Member States participate in the voting procedure and the number of votes is distributed across the 28 Member States. The total number of votes is 352 and the number apportioned to each Member State ranges from 29 for Germany, France and the UK to 3 for Malta.

Distribution of votes for each Member State

Germany, France, Italy, United Kingdom	29
Spain, Poland	27
Romania	14
Netherlands	13
Belgium, Czech Republic, Greece, Hungary, Portugal	12
Austria, Bulgaria, Sweden	10
Denmark, Ireland, Lithuania, Slovakia, Finland, Croatia	7
Cyprus, Estonia, Latvia, Luxembourg, Slovenia	4
Malta	3
TOTAL	352

In certain circumstances one or more of the Member States will not participate in the vote because they have negotiated an 'opt-out' on the matter being decided. If fewer than 28 Member States are voting, the voting requirements will be adjusted accordingly.

[2.10] The different types of voting are as follows:

Unanimity

This method of voting requires the agreement of all the Member States. As a result the unanimity procedure can be a slow process and each Member State has the power to block a decision. Unanimity voting applies to key areas such as membership of the Union.

Simple Majority

Simple majority was the voting system until the Lisbon Treaty was ratified. According to Art 16(3) TFEU the Council shall act by a qualified majority except where the Treaties provide otherwise.

Qualified Majority

Until 30 October 2014, the system in operation in the Council was the qualified majority voting system.

A qualified majority is reached if there are at least 260 votes cast in favour or a majority of the 28 Member States vote in favour. A Member State may ask for confirmation that the votes in favour represent at least 62 per cent of the EU population and if this percentage is not confirmed the proposal will not be passed.

Double Majority

Double Majority will be the new voting system from 1 November 2014.

This voting system requires two types of majority in order for a proposal to be passed. Firstly, there must be a majority of at least 15 Member States and secondly, the majority must represent at least 65 per cent of the population of the European Union.

According to Protocol 36 of the TFEU, between November 2014 and March 2017 any Member State in the Council may request that the system of qualified majority voting is to be used in place of the new double majority voting system.

[2.11] When the Council acts on a proposal by the Commission or the High Representative of the Union for Foreign Affairs and Security Policy, a double majority decision will be adopted once 55 per cent or more of the Member States vote in favour and they represent at least 65 per cent of the population of the EU. In order to block a proposal, at least four Council Member States representing 35 per cent of the EU population would have to oppose the proposal.

When the Council does not act on a proposal from the Commission or the High Representative, a double majority decision will be adopted once 72 per cent or more of the Council Members vote in favour and they represent at least 65 per cent of the population of the EU.

The Committee of Permanent Representatives (COREPER)

[2.12] The Committee of Permanent Representatives, known as COREPER, prepares and co-ordinates the work of the Council. The Committee consists of permanent representatives from the governments of the Member States.

The work of the Committee is divided into two working groups COREPER I and COREPER II.

COREPER I is comprised of the Deputy Permanent Representatives and it prepares the work for the following Council configurations:

- Employment, Social Policy, Health and Consumer Affairs;
- Competitiveness (internal market, industry, research and tourism);
- Transport, Telecommunications and Energy;
- Agriculture and Fisheries;
- Environment; and
- Education, Youth and Culture (including audiovisual).

COREPER II is comprised of the Permanent Representatives and it prepares the work for the following configurations:

- General Affairs and External Relations (including European security and defence policy and development cooperation);

- Economic and Financial Affairs (including the budget); and

- Justice and Home Affairs (including civil protection).

THE COMMISSION

[2.13] The seat of the Commission is Brussels, Belgium.

The Commission represents the interests of the European Union and it is independent of the Member States and the National Governments. Each Member State has one Commissioner.

The Commission brings actions against Member States or individuals who are in breach of EU Law. It also implements EU policies, proposes legislation and allocates EU funds.

The Commission comprises:

- The President of the Commission;

- The High Representative of the Union for Foreign Affairs and Security Policy (Art 18(4) TEU); and

- The Commissioners.

The European Council nominates the President of the Commission and the President is then elected by the European Parliament.

The Treaty of Lisbon established the new role of High Representative of the Union for Foreign Affairs and Security Policy and is appointed by the European Council and the President of the Commission. The High Representative conducts the European Union's common foreign and security policy and has a dual function, being one of the Vice Presidents of the Commission as well as a representative for the Council.

The Commissioners are selected from a list of recommendations made by the Member States. Article 17(3) TEU outlines the criteria for selection and states that

> 'The members of the Commission shall be chosen on the ground of their general competence and European commitment from persons whose independence is beyond doubt'.

[2.14] There are currently 28 Commissioners, one representing each Member State. The number of Commissioners has been addressed by the amending treaties. The Treaty of Nice stated that when the European Union reached a membership of 27 the number of Commissioners must be less than the number of Member States. This provision was to take affect by June 2009.

The Treaty of Lisbon attempted to extend this provision by stating in Art 17(5) TEU that

> 'As from 1 November 2014, the Commission shall consist of a number of members, including its President and the High Representative of the Union for Foreign Affairs and Security Policy, corresponding to two thirds of the number of Member States, unless the European Council, acting unanimously, decides to alter this number'.

[2.15] However in 2008, Ireland held the first referendum on the Lisbon Treaty and the Treaty was rejected by the Irish citizens. Following the Irish rejection of the Lisbon Treaty negotiations took place and one of the issues highlighted was the loss of an Irish Commissioner. In order to secure a positive vote from the Irish citizens in the second referendum on the Lisbon Treaty the European Council addressed this issue. At a meeting of the European Council in December 2008 it was agreed that

> 'On the composition of the Commission, the European Council recalls that the Treaties currently in force require that the number of Commissioners be reduced in 2009. The European Council agrees that provided the Treaty of Lisbon enters into force, a decision will be taken, in accordance with the necessary legal procedures, to the effect that the

Commission shall continue to include one national of each Member State'.

The Irish citizens accepted the Lisbon Treaty in the second referendum held in 2009. Due to the fact that the Lisbon Treaty has now entered into force the number of Commissioners will remain at one per Member State. However the number of Commissioners can be reduced if the European Council agrees unanimously to do so. In 2013 the accession of Croatia to the European Union raised the number of Commissioners to 28.

Appointment and Removal of the Commissioners

[2.16] The President, the High Representative and the Commissioners are subject to the approval of the European Parliament. Following this approval the new Commission is then appointed by the European Council.

Pursuant to Art 17(3) TEU the Commissioners are appointed for a renewable five-year term. The European Parliament has the power to remove the Commission in its entirety if a motion of censure is passed (Art 234 TEU). However, the European Parliament cannot remove individual Commissioners.

Article 247 TFEU states that if a Member of the Commission no longer fulfils the conditions required for the performance of his duties or if he has been guilty of serious misconduct, the Court of Justice may, on application by the Council acting by a simple majority or the Commission, compulsorily retire him.

Article 17(6) TEU states that a member of the Commission shall resign if the President so requests.

Powers and Functions of the Commission

[2.17] Article 17(6) TEU contains the powers of the President of the Commission. Accordingly, the President shall:

(a) lay down guidelines within which the Commission is to work;

(b) decide on the internal organisation of the Commission, ensuring that it acts consistently, efficiently and as a collegiate body; and

(c) appoint Vice-Presidents, other than the High Representative of the Union for Foreign Affairs and Security Policy, from among the members of the Commission.

The President also allocates portfolios to the Commissioners.

The powers of the Commission are contained in Art 17(1) TEU and are as follows:

(a) The Commission shall promote the general interest of the Union and take appropriate initiatives to that end;

(b) It shall ensure the application of the Treaties, and of measures adopted by the institutions pursuant to them;

(c) It shall oversee the application of Union law under the control of the Court of Justice of the European Union;

(d) It shall execute the budget and manage programmes;

(e) It shall exercise coordinating, executive and management functions, as laid down in the Treaties;

(f) With the exception of the common foreign and security policy, and other cases provided for in the Treaties, it shall ensure the Union's external representation;

(g) It shall initiate the Union's annual and multiannual programming with a view to achieving interinstitutional agreements.

The Commission also has a legislative function which will be discussed in more detail in **Ch 4**.

THE COURT OF JUSTICE OF THE EUROPEAN UNION

[2.18] The EU courts are located in Luxembourg City, Luxembourg.

According to Art 19 TEU, the Court of Justice of the European Union includes the Court of Justice, the General Court and the specialised courts. The General Court was formerly known as the Court of First Instance. The specialised courts were formerly known as the judicial panels.

The Court of Justice of the European Union ensures that EU law is observed when the treaties are interpreted and applied.

The Court of Justice

[2.19] The Court of Justice consists of 28 judges, one from each Member State.

According to Art 19(3) TEU the jurisdiction of the Court of Justice is to;

(a) rule on actions brought by a Member State, an institution or a natural legal person (this includes direct actions for annulment, failure of a Member State to fulfil an obligation and actions against institutions for failure to act, see **Ch 7**).

(b) give preliminary rulings, at the request of courts or tribunals of the Member States, on the interpretation of Union law or the validity of acts adopted by the institutions (see **Ch 6**).

(c) rule in other cases provided for in the Treaties (this includes disputes relating to compensation for damage provided for in the second and third paragraphs of Art 340 TEU).The appellate jurisdiction of the Court of Justice is outlined in Art 256 TFEU, which provides that the Court of Justice may hear appeals on a point of law from the General Court. In exceptional circumstances the Court of Justice may review the determinations of the General Court in proceedings brought against the decisions of the specialised courts.

The Court of Justice has used its jurisdiction to develop EU law. For example, the principles of direct effect and supremacy are not contained in the treaties and these principles were developed by the Court utilising its jurisdiction.

The work of the court is assisted by nine advocates-general. This number can be increased at the Council's request. The advocates-general assist the court by giving reasoned opinions but they do not participate in the court's deliberations. The purpose of the advocates-general opinion is to provide a legal solution for the different cases before the court. Although the opinion is not binding on the court, it is considered to be very important. The court will only request an opinion for new developments in EU Law.

The judges and advocates general are appointed for six years. According to Art 253 TFEU, the judges and advocates-general of the Court of Justice shall be chosen from persons whose independence is beyond doubt and who possess the qualifications required for appointment to the highest judicial offices in their respective countries or who are jurisconsults of recognised competence. They are appointed by common accord of the governments of the Member States, after consultation with a panel comprising of former members of the Court of Justice and the General Court, members of national supreme courts and lawyers of recognised competence.

The General Court

[2.20] The General Court (formerly known as the Court of First Instance) was created to assist the Court of Justice by reducing its case load. The number of judges of the General Court shall be determined by the Statute of the Court of Justice of the European Union. There are currently 28 judges of the General Court, as determined by statute. However, there are no permanent advocates general at the General Court, a judge may be appointed to carry out the work of an advocate general for complex cases.

The General Court has jurisdiction to hear direct actions for annulment, actions for failure to act and damages actions. The General Court can also give preliminary rulings in specific areas laid down by statute and it can hear appeals brought against decisions of the specialised courts. The preliminary rulings and appeals can be reviewed by the Court of Justice in exceptional circumstances and only under the conditions and within the limits laid down by the statute, where there is a serious risk of the unity or consistency of Union law being affected.

The Specialised Courts

[2.21] The specialised courts were formerly known as judicial panels. These specialised courts are set up by the Council. The European Civil Service Tribunal is the first of these specialised courts and it was established in order to hear cases between the European Union and its Civil Service.

The European Civil Service Tribunal consists of seven judges who are chosen by lottery. Decisions of specialised courts can be appealed to the General Court and additional specialised courts may be established in the future.

THE COURT OF AUDITORS

[2.22] The Court of Auditors monitors the revenue and expenditure accounts of the European Union. The Court of Auditors consists of 28 members, one national from each Member State. The members are appointed for six years. Pursuant to Art 286 TFEU:

> 'The Members of the Court of Auditors shall be chosen from among persons who belong or have belonged in their respective States to external audit bodies or who are especially qualified for this office'.

The Court of Auditors provides the European Parliament and Council with a statement of assurance as to the reliability of the accounts and the legality and regularity of the underlying transactions and this is published in the Official Journal of the European Union (Art 287 TFEU).

THE EUROPEAN COUNCIL

[2.23] It should be noted that the European Council and the Council of Ministers are two separate entities. The role of the Council of Ministers was dealt with earlier in this chapter.

The European Council consists of the heads of state from the governments of the Member States, together with its President and the President of the Commission. The High Representative of the Union for Foreign Affairs and Security Policy also takes part in its work.

The European Council provides the Union with the necessary impetus for its development and it outlines the general political directions and priorities of the Union (Art 15 TEU) but it does not exercise legislative functions. It meets twice every six months.

According to Art 15(5), TEU the European Council shall elect a President by a qualified majority, for a term of two and a half years, renewable once.

The President's duties are set out in Art 15(6) and are as follows:

(a) to chair the European Council and drive forward its work;

(b) to ensure the preparation and continuity of the work of the European Council in cooperation with the President of the Commission, and on the basis of the work of the General Affairs Council;

(c) to endeavour to facilitate cohesion and consensus within the European Council;

(d) to present a report to the European Parliament after each of the meetings of the European Council.

The President of the European Council shall, at his level and in that capacity, ensure the external representation of the Union on issues concerning its common foreign and security policy, without prejudice to the powers of the High Representative of the Union for Foreign Affairs and Security Policy. The President of the European Council is not permitted to hold a national office.

THE EUROPEAN CENTRAL BANK

[2.24] The European Central Bank and the national central banks, together, constitute the European System of Central Banks (ESCB). The primary objective of the ESCB is to maintain price stability.

The European Central Bank is an independent body and it alone authorises the issue of the euro. According to Art 282 TFEU, the European Central Bank shall be consulted on all proposed Union acts, and all proposals for regulation at national level, and may give an opinion on matters that fall within its responsibilities.

Chapter 3

Sources of Law

INTRODUCTION

[3.01] The legal system that exists in the European Union is made up of different sources of law. The sources of law are:

- Primary legislation: The Treaty on the Functioning of the European Union (TFEU) and The Treaty on the European Union (TEU), as amended by the Lisbon Treaty are the primary sources of EU Law.

- Secondary legislation: regulations, directives, decisions, recommendations and opinions.

- International agreements.

- Case law of the Court of Justice.

- The general principles of EU law.

PRIMARY LEGISLATION

[3.02] The primary source of EU law is found in the treaties. The treaties contain the primary objectives, laws and institutional framework of the European Union. The Court of Justice interprets the treaties and ensures the correct application of EU law. Treaty provisions are directly applicable, this means that they automatically become part of national law and no action is required for their enactment.

SECONDARY LEGISLATION

[3.03] The European institutions enact secondary legislation in order to give effect to the contents of the treaties. Secondary legislation includes regulations, directives and decisions which are binding, and recommendations and opinions which are non-binding.

Regulations

[3.04] A regulation has general application which means that it is binding in its entirety and directly applicable in all Member States. Regulations do not need national legislation to be implemented and apply to governments, institutions and individuals.

Article 297 TFEU states that regulations must be published in the Official Journal of the European Union and must enter into force on the date specified in them or, in the absence thereof, on the twentieth day following that of their publication.

Directives

[3.05] Article 288 TFEU states that a directive is binding, as to the result to be achieved, upon each Member State to which it is addressed, but shall leave to the national authorities the choice of form and methods.

Member States are required to implement directives. Directives are drafted in general terms and Member States are required to implement them within a specific time frame. Directives are not directly applicable and Member States have discretion to choose the means by which the objectives of the directive are met.

Article 297 TFEU states that directives must be published in the Official Journal of the European Union and they must enter into force on the date specified in them or, in the absence thereof, on the twentieth day following that of their publication.

Decisions

[3.06] Decisions are addressed to Member States or to particular individuals. Decisions are binding in their entirety but if the decision is addressed to a particular person it is only binding on the person to whom it is addressed.

Recommendations and Opinions

[3.07] Recommendations and opinions do not have binding force and cannot establish rights and obligations directly. They merely provide guidance on the interpretation and content of EU law.

International Agreements

[3.08] The European Union can enter into international agreements. The EU institutions and Member States are bound by the international agreements entered into by the European Union.

Case Law of the Court of Justice

[3.09] The decisions of the Court of Justice of the European Union (CJEU) are binding on all Member States and their national courts.

The General Principles of EU Law

[3.10] General principles are unwritten principles of law that have been developed by the Court of Justice of the European Union. The principles come from the common constitutional traditions of the EU Member States and are binding on the EU institutions and Member States. General principles include:

- proportionality;
- legitimate expectation;
- non-discrimination; and
- transparency.

General principles allow the Court of Justice to interpret and expand EU law and EU law can be challenged on the basis that a piece of law is contrary to a general principle.

Fundamental rights are also general principles of EU law. The area of fundamental rights saw two major developments following the coming into force of the Lisbon Treaty:

1   The EU Charter of Fundamental Rights has the same status as the treaties and is binding on the Member States and the Court of Justice.

2   Article 6(2) TEU provides for the accession of the EU to the European Convention on Human Rights.

Chapter 4

The Law-Making Process

INTRODUCTION

[4.01] The Commission, the Council and the Parliament all play different roles in creating EU legislation. The legislative procedures used to vary according to the policy area or the nature of the potential legislation.

The Lisbon Treaty made a number of changes to the EU legislative procedures. Prior to the Lisbon Treaty coming into force the main legislative procedures were, co-decision, co-operation, consultation and assent. However the law-making process in the EU was often criticised as being undemocratic and the Lisbon Treaty addressed and remedied some of these concerns. Co-decision has been renamed the ordinary legislative procedure. Consultation and assent continue to operate in limited situations under the special legislative procedure. The co-operation procedure no longer exists.

THE ORDINARY LEGISLATIVE PROCEDURE

[4.02] The ordinary legislative procedure was introduced by the TEU. The provisions outlining how the procedure operates are now contained in Art 294 TFEU. The ordinary legislative procedure gives the Parliament more power in the legislative process. However, the Commission continues to initiate EU legislation.

The following is an outline of the ordinary legislative procedure as contained in Art 294 TFEU.

1. Where reference is made in the treaties to the ordinary legislative procedure for the adoption of an act, the following procedure shall apply.

2.   The Commission shall submit a proposal to the European Parliament and the Council.

First reading

[4.03]

3.   The European Parliament shall adopt its position at first reading and communicate it to the Council.

4.   If the Council approves the European Parliament's position, the act concerned shall be adopted in the wording which corresponds to the position of the European Parliament.

5.   If the Council does not approve the European Parliament's position, it shall adopt its position at first reading and communicate it to the European Parliament.

6.   The Council shall inform the European Parliament fully of the reasons which led it to adopt its position at first reading. The Commission shall inform the European Parliament fully of its position.

Second reading

[4.04]

7.   If, within three months of such communication, the European Parliament:

  (a)   approves the Council's position at first reading or has not taken a decision, the act concerned shall be deemed to have been adopted in the wording which corresponds to the position of the Council;

  (b)   rejects, by a majority of its component members, the Council's position at first reading, the proposed act shall be deemed not to have been adopted;

(c) proposes, by a majority of its component members, amendments to the Council's position at first reading, the text thus amended shall be forwarded to the Council and to the Commission, which shall deliver an opinion on those amendments.

8. If, within three months of receiving the European Parliament's amendments, the Council, acting by a qualified majority:

(a) approves all those amendments, the act in question shall be deemed to have been adopted;

(b) does not approve all the amendments, the President of the Council, in agreement with the President of the European Parliament, shall within six weeks convene a meeting of the Conciliation Committee.

9. The Council must vote unanimously on the amendments on which the Commission has delivered a negative opinion.

Conciliation

[4.05]

10. The Conciliation Committee, which shall be composed of the members of the Council or their representatives and an equal number of members representing the European Parliament, shall have the task of reaching agreement on a joint text, by a qualified majority of the members of the Council or their representatives and by a majority of the members representing the European Parliament within six weeks of its being convened, on the basis of the positions of the European Parliament and the Council at second reading.

11. The Commission shall take part in the Conciliation Committee's proceedings and shall take all necessary initiatives with a view to reconciling the positions of the European Parliament and the Council.

12. If, within six weeks of its being convened, the Conciliation Committee does not approve the joint text, the proposed act shall be deemed not to have been adopted.

Third reading

[4.06]

13. If, within that period, the Conciliation Committee approves a joint text, the European Parliament, acting by a majority of the votes cast, and the Council, acting by a qualified majority, shall each have a period of six weeks from that approval in which to adopt the act in question in accordance with the joint text. If they fail to do so, the proposed act shall be deemed not to have been adopted.

14. The periods of three months and six weeks referred to in this Article shall be extended by a maximum of one month and two weeks respectively at the initiative of the European Parliament or the Council.

Special provisions

[4.07]

15. Where, in the cases provided for in the treaties, a legislative act is submitted to the ordinary legislative procedure on the initiative of a group of Member States, on a recommendation by the European Central Bank, or at the request of the Court of Justice, para 2, the second sentence of para 6 and para 9 shall not apply.

    In such cases, the European Parliament and the Council shall communicate the proposed act to the Commission with their positions at first and second readings. The European Parliament or the Council may request the opinion of the Commission throughout the procedure, which the Commission may also deliver on its own initiative. It may also, if it deems it necessary, take part in the Conciliation Committee in accordance with para 11.

Adopting Legislation

[4.08] The European Parliament and Council jointly approve the final text of a legislative proposal and it is then signed by the Presidents and Secretaries General of the two institutions. Once signed the legislation is published in the Official Journal.

The proposal will not be adopted if at any point during the procedure it is rejected or the Parliament and Council cannot reach a compromise. If this occurs the procedure will be ended. The Commission can start a new procedure with a new proposal.

THE SPECIAL LEGISLATIVE PROCEDURE

[4.09] The special legislative procedure was introduced by the Lisbon Treaty. Article 289(2) TFEU defines the special legislative procedure as the adoption of legislation by the Parliament with the participation of the Council or the adoption of legislation by the Council with the participation of the Parliament.

The consultation and assent procedures were replaced by the special legislative procedure. However they still operate in certain situations as outlined by the Lisbon Treaty.

Consultation

[4.10] The consultation procedure is starts with the Commission submitting a proposal on legislation to the Council. The Council then consults with the Parliament on the proposed piece of legislation. The Parliament's role is minimal and any opinions expressed by the Parliament have no binding force. However the consultation with the Parliament is an essential procedural requirement and failure to do so constitutes a ground for annulment of the legislation.

The consultation procedure is now only used in limited situations due to the fact that greater importance is being placed on the Parliament's involvement. The use of the consultation procedure can be seen in Art 22 TFEU on citizens' rights in municipal elections and Art 115 TFEU on the establishment or functioning of the internal market.

Consent (formerly Assent)

[4.11] This procedure was introduced by the SEA and operates as follows. The Council is required to obtain the Parliament's consent before certain decisions can be passed. The Parliament may only accept or reject a proposal. The Parliament does not offer an opinion and there is no facility to amend the proposal. In order for the Parliament to accept a proposal there must be an absolute majority of votes.

Examples of when consent is required are as follows:

- Under Art 7 TEU when there is a serious breach of fundamental rights;
- When a decision has to be made on the admission of new members to the EU; and
- Under Art 19 TFEU where a decision is made to combat discrimination based on sex, racial or ethnic origin, religion or belief, disability, age or sexual orientation.

Chapter 5

Supremacy

INTRODUCTION

[5.01] The treaty provisions, secondary legislation and the case law of the Court of Justice are all part of the body of law referred to as EU law. EU law represents a completely new legal order that has been created and developed since the 1950s.

When Member States join the European Union they limit their sovereignty and accept the precedence of EU law. National law and EU law operate side by side in the Member States. However, national law and EU law are two different bodies of law and differences often emerge. The doctrine of supremacy (primacy) was developed by the Court of Justice to address the situation where there is a conflict between national law and EU law. The meaning of supremacy is that EU Law has primacy over national law. Therefore, EU Law will prevail if there is a conflict between national law and EU law.

The doctrine of supremacy ensures the correct application of EU law. However, supremacy is not expressly referred to in the treaties. The Court of Justice created and developed the doctrine through its case law.

[5.02] The first official reference to supremacy was made in Declaration No 17 of the Lisbon Treaty. It states the following;

> 'The Conference recalls that, in accordance with well settled case law of the Court of Justice of the European Union, the Treaties and the law adopted by the Union on the basis of the Treaties have primacy over the law of Member States, under the conditions laid down by the said case law.'

An Opinion of the Council Legal Service of the 22 June 2007 is also attached to the Lisbon Treaty. It states the following;

> 'It results from the case-law of the Court of Justice that primacy of EC law is a cornerstone principle of Community law. According to the Court, this principle is inherent to the specific nature of the European Community. At the time of the first judgment of this established case law (*Costa/ENEL*, 15 July 1964, Case 6/64) there was no mention of primacy in the treaty. It is still the case today. The fact that the principle of primacy will not be included in the future treaty shall not in any way change the existence of the principle and the existing case-law of the Court of Justice.'

CASE LAW ON SUPREMACY

[5.03] The doctrine of supremacy is not contained in the treaties and it has been developed through the decisions of the Court of Justice.

In *Van Gend en Loos* (Case 26/62), [1963] ECR 1 the court stated that 'the Community constitutes a new legal order of international law for the benefit of which the states have limited there sovereign rights'.

The doctrine of supremacy was established in *Costa v ENEL* (Case C–6/64), [1964] ECR 585. This case involved a piece of Italian legislation that had been enacted subsequent to the EEC Treaty. As a result the Italian government argued that the Court of Justice did not have jurisdiction to hear the preliminary reference. The Court of Justice did not agree with this argument and outlined the basis for the supremacy of EU law. The court stated that EU law had been integrated into the Member States' legal systems and as a result was binding on them. The court also stated that EU law was of unlimited duration, it had autonomous power and Member States had limited their competence by accepting the treaties.

The court went on to say that Member States had accepted a new legal order and this was a permanent limitation on their sovereign rights. As a result Member States were unable to establish a body of national law contrary to EU law. The court also referred to Art 249 EC (now Art 288 TFEU) that provides regulations are binding and directly applicable in all Member States. The court held that this article would be meaningless if Member States could enact legislation which was inconsistent with EU law.

[5.04] The doctrine of supremacy was explained further in *Internationale Handelsgesellschaft GmbH* (Case 11/70), [1970] ECR 1125. In this case a system imposed under EC regulations breached freedoms enshrined in the German constitution. As a result the German court believed that the piece of EC legislation was unconstitutional. The Court of Justice held that EU law must take precedence over national law. In addition, national courts have an obligation to set aside any national provisions that conflict with EU law. This obligation applies to all forms of national law even a constitutional principle.

In *Simmenthal* (Case 106/77), [1978] ECR 629 an Italian court asked the Court of Justice for guidance on how to apply a piece of Italian legislation that was violating EU law. It had been previously decided by the Court of Justice that the piece of Italian legislation was violating EU law. However the necessary steps to repeal the piece of legislation had not been taken by the Italian constitutional court. The Court of Justice held that every national court has an obligation to apply EU law in its entirety and any conflicting national law must be set aside.

In *Factortame II* (Case C–213/89), [1990] ECR I–2433 an application for an interim injunction was brought in a UK court. The applicants were seeking an interim injunction to set aside certain provisions of the UK Merchant Shipping Act 1988. According to the UK doctrine of parliamentary sovereignty, an Act of Parliament could not be suspended by a court. The Court of Justice held that 'Community law must be interpreted as meaning that a national court which, in a case before it concerning Community law, considers that the sole obstacle which precludes it from granting interim relief is a rule of national law must set aside that rule'.

INCORPORATION OF EU LAW IN IRELAND

[5.05] EU law represents a completely new legal order and as a result it must be incorporated into the Member States' national legal systems. For Ireland membership of the European Union required amendments to the Irish Constitution and the enactment of new legislation.

Article 29 of the Irish Constitution contains the provisions on international relations. Article 29.4.6° acknowledges Irish membership of the European Union and states the following;

> 'No provision of this Constitution invalidates laws enacted, acts done or measures adopted by the State, before, on or after the entry into force of the Treaty of Lisbon, that are necessitated by the obligations of membership of the European Union referred to in subsection 5° of this section or of the European Atomic Energy Community, or prevents laws enacted, acts done or measures adopted by—
>
> I.   the said European Union or the European Atomic Energy Community, or institutions thereof,
>
> II.   the European Communities or European Union existing immediately before the entry into force of the Treaty of Lisbon, or institutions thereof, or
>
> III.   bodies competent under the treaties referred to in this section, from having the force of law in the State.'

The amendments to the Irish Constitution provide EU law with immunity from constitutional challenge and EU law automatically becomes law in Ireland. Article 29.4.6° applies to two types of legislation:

1   legislation that is enacted by the EU Institutions; and

2   legislation that is enacted by the Irish State in order to comply with EU law.

[5.06] The constitutional amendments are supplemented by national legislation. Due to the evolving nature of the European Union the provisions contained in national legislation are regularly updated and amended.

Section 2(1) of the European Communities Act 1972 (as amended by the European Communities Act 1992) states;

> "From the 1st day of January, 1973, the treaties governing the European Communities and the existing and future acts adopted by the institutions of those Communities shall be binding on the State and shall be part of the domestic law thereof under the conditions laid down in those treaties."

Section 2 of the European Communities Act 1972 has been amended by s 3 of the European Union Act 2009 that states:

> '(1) The following shall be binding on the State and shall be part of the domestic law thereof under the conditions laid down in the treaties governing the European Union:
>
> (a)   the treaties governing the European Union;
>
> (b)   acts adopted by the institutions of the European Union ...;
>
> (c)   acts adopted by the institutions of the European Communities in force immediately before the entry into force of the Lisbon Treaty; and
>
> (d)   acts adopted by bodies competent under those Treaties ....'

Section 3 of The European Communities Act 1972 empowers Irish Ministers to implement EU Law. Section 3(1) allows a Minister to make regulations in order to give effect to s 2. As a result approval from the Oireachtas is not required in order for a piece of EU law to be transposed into Irish national law.

The European Communities Act 2007 was enacted to amend s 3 of the European Communities Act 1972. The new piece of legislation increases ministerial powers.

Section 2 of the 2007 Act amends s 3 of the European Communities Act 1972 and states that the regulations under this section may:

> '(a)   make provision for offences under the regulations to be prosecuted on indictment, where the Minister of the

Government making the regulations considers it necessary for the purpose of giving effect to:

(1)   a provision that the treaties constrain the European Communities, or

(2)   an act or provision of an act, adopted by an institution of the European Communities or any other body competent under those treaties; and

(b)   makes such provisions as that Minister of the Government considers necessary for the purpose of ensuring that penalties in respect of an offence prosecuted in that manner are effective and proportionate, and have a deterrent effect, having regard to the acts or omissions of which the offences consists...'

Section 4 of the 2007 Act states that:

'(1) A power to make a statutory instrument conferred on a Minister of the Government by a provision of a statute may be exercised for the purpose of giving effect to a European act if the obligations imposed on the State under the European act concerned relate, in whole, to matters to which that provision relates.

(2) A statutory instrument made for the purpose referred to in sub-section 1 may contain such incidental, supplementary and consequential provisions as appear to the Minister of the Government making the statutory instrument to be necessary for the purposes of the statutory instrument (including provisions repealing, amending or applying, with or without modification, other law, exclusive of this Act, the Act of 1972 and the provision of the statute under which the statutory instrument is made).'

The Minister was to be given far-reaching powers in this new piece of legislation. The new powers are intended to have a practical purpose. However the far-reaching nature is questionable.

[5.07] In the case of *McCauley Chemists Blackpool Limited v Pharmaceutical Society of Ireland* (31 July 2002) HC, (Case C–221/05), 2006 ECR 1/6869 the plaintiff challenged the validity of the

statutory instrument that implemented Council Directive 85/433/
EEC on the mutual recognition of pharmacist qualifications. The
directive placed foreign pharmacists at an unfair advantage and the
directive was implemented in Ireland, the statutory instrument
corresponding to the directive word for word. In the Supreme Court
a question was sent to the Court of Justice asking whether or not the
directive conferred a discretion on Member States. The Court of
Justice held when interpreting Art 2 of Council Directive 85/433/
EEC that a Member State who complied merely with the minimal
level of recognition laid down in the directive was not exercising any
discretion conferred by that directive.

International Law

[5.08] The European Union enjoys a unique position under Irish law
and EU law automatically applies in Ireland. Article 29 of the Irish
Constitution and the European Communities Acts provide that EU
law can be enforced in Ireland without a need for national
legislation. As a result, EU law is not classified in the same way as
international law.

International law does not become part of Irish law automatically
and a piece of international law can only be relied upon in an Irish
court when the international law has been incorporated into Irish law
by the Oireachtas. Ireland is a dualist state and as such it regards
international law as being completely separate from national law
(see further **Ch 17** Fundamental Rights).

European Union law is a unique exception to Ireland's position as a
dualist state.

Irish Case Law on Supremacy

[5.09] If there is conflict between Irish constitutional law and EU
law, EU law will always prevail. *In Campus Oil v Minister for
Industry and Energy (No 2)* 1983 IR 88 the Supreme Court held that
European Union law will always take precedence even over the
provisions of the Irish Constitution. The supremacy of EU law over

Irish constitutional law is protected by Art 29 of the Irish Constitution.

Any piece of legislation that is enacted by the EU institutions is immune from a challenge of constitutionality. Therefore, EU law is automatically part of Irish law even if it is in contradiction with the terms of the Irish Constitution.

Delegated Legislation and EU Law

[5.10] Article 15.2.1° of the Irish Constitution states that only the Oireachtas can create laws. It provides as follows:

> 'The sole and exclusive power of making laws for the State is hereby vested in the Oireachtas: no other legislative authority has power to make laws for the State'.

Article 29.4.6° of the Irish Constitution limits the effect of Art 15.2.1° and it permits the European Union to make laws that apply in the Irish State. Article 29.4.6° states:

> 'No provision of this Constitution invalidates laws enacted, acts done or measures adopted by the State, before, on or after the entry into force of the Treaty of Lisbon, that are necessitated by the obligations of membership of the European Union ...'.

The result of the constitutional provisions is that a piece of EU legislation can become law in the Irish State even though the Oireachtas has not incorporated the piece of EU legislation.

[5.11] It is not possible for the Oireachtas to enact every piece of legislation and as a result the Oireachtas must delegate some of its law-making power to other bodies. In Ireland delegated legislation takes the form of statutory instruments. Statutory instruments are normally technical in nature and are also adopted by Government ministers in order to implement EU legislation.

In order to be lawful delegated legislation must not exceed the provisions of the 'principles and policies' test and it must not become actual law making. If delegated legislation becomes law making this would be unconstitutional as according to Article 15.2.1° of the Irish Constitution law making is something that only the Oireachtas can do.

[5.12] To put an end to any uncertainty the Irish courts have clarified the position on how delegated legislation is to be treated. The Government can engage in adopting statutory instruments once certain conditions are satisfied. Firstly, the 'principles and policies' test must be applied. Secondly, the statutory instrument cannot change or amend the law.

The principles and policies test was established in the case of *Cityview Press v An Coimhairle Oiliuna (AnCO)* 1980 IR 381. In this case the plaintiff challenged the validity of delegated legislation. The court set out when delegated legislation would be valid and the decision is now known as the 'principles and policies' test. The court stated:

> 'The test is whether that which is challenged as an unauthorised delegation of parliamentary power is more than a mere giving effect to 'principles and policies' which are contained in the statute itself. If it be, then it is not authorised; for such would constitute a purported exercise of legislative power by an authority which is not permitted to do so under the Constitution. On the other hand, if it be within the permitted limits – if the law is laid down in the statute and details only are filled in or completed by the designated Minister or subordinate body – there is no unauthorised delegation of legislative power'.

This 'principles and policies' test created by the Supreme Court in the *Cityview* case also applies to delegated EU legislation. The case law in this area has provided guidance on the implementation of delegated EU legislation.

In *Meagher v Minister for Agriculture* [1994] 1 IR 329 the Minister altered the Petty Sessions Act, 1851 by implementing an EC directive pursuant to s 3 of the European Communities Act 1972. The plaintiff argued that only the Oireachtas could change legislation and as a result the ministerial power to change legislation was unconstitutional. The Supreme Court held that the process whereby Ministers transposed directives into national law was 'necessary' in order to fulfil Ireland's EU law obligations. The court stated that it would be impossible to implement every EU directive by an Act of the Oireachtas due to the high volume of directives and Ireland would not meet its obligation under EU law if it failed to implement all the directives.

[5.13] The Supreme Court provided further clarification in the case of *Maher v Minister for Agriculture* [2001] 2 IR 139. In this case the Supreme Court considered the implementation of an EU regulation through secondary legislation. The Minister had implemented a Council regulation on milk quotas into Irish law by adopting a statutory instrument. The plaintiff argued that the implementation process was contrary to Art 15.2 of the Irish Constitution. The Supreme Court held that the process of implementation by statutory instrument was lawful as the Minister was merely giving effect to the principles and policies already contained in EU legislation. However, this process can only be used when the EU legislation contains the policies. If the EU legislation allows Member States to make the policy decisions then a statutory instrument is not sufficient and an Act of the Oireactas is required.

An Act of the Oireachtas is required if the piece of EU law leaves a discretion as to principles and policies with the Member State. Directives and regulations normally clearly state the exact principles and policies. In these circumstances a Minister is only giving effect to the principles and policies of EU law. If a piece of EU law does not clearly state the principle and policy an Act of the Oireachtas is required.

[5.14] Irish courts have also considered the interaction between the doctrine of supremacy and the fundamental rights provisions of the Irish Constitution. Article 40.3.3° of the Irish Constitution protects the life of the unborn and its provisions came under scrutiny in *Society for the Protection of Unborn Children (SPUC) v Grogan* [1989] IR 713 students had been distributing information on how to obtain abortion services in the UK. The plaintiff, SPUC, sought an injunction to prevent the defendant from distributing the information. A preliminary reference was sent to the Court of Justice asking if the freedom to provide a service under EU law had been breached. The Court of Justice stated that abortion services came within the definition of a service under Art 50 EC (now Art 57 TFEU). However the information was distributed by students who were not remunerated for their work and consequently the distribution did not come within the meaning of Art 49 EC (now Art 56 TFEU). As a result the Court of Justice did not give a ruling. This case highlights the difficulties that can arise between EU law and the fundamental rights provisions in the Irish Constitution.

The importance of Article 40.3.3° was recognised in Protocol No 35 to the TEU and TFEU, which states the following;

> 'Nothing in the Treaties, or in the Treaty establishing the European Atomic Energy Community, or in the Treaties or Acts modifying or supplementing those Treaties, shall affect the application in Ireland of Article 40.3.3° of the Constitution of Ireland.'

Irish Constitutional Amendments and New EU Treaties

[5.15] The EU has developed rapidly since it first came into existence post World War II. In response to these developments the EU has introduced new treaties. These new treaties contain the updated and amended the goals and objectives of the European Union and there have been many these amending treaties such as the Single European Act, the Maastricht Treaty, the Nice Treaty and the Lisbon Treaty.

A new treaty will not come into force until every Member State of the European Union has ratified the new treaty. The Irish State decides whether or not to ratify a new EU treaty by holding a referendum. As a result, it is the Irish people who decide whether or not an EU treaty will be ratified in Ireland. The need for a referendum was identified in the case of *Crotty v An Taoiseach* [1987] IR 713.

In *Crotty,* the plaintiff argued that the State did not have power to ratify the Single European Act (SEA) unless the Constitution was amended. The plaintiff's argument was based on Title III of the SEA which related to European co-operation in the area of foreign policy. The Supreme Court held that Title III of the SEA could not be ratified without constitutional amendment. The court's decision was based on the fact that the ratification of Title III of the SEA was not necessary in order to meet the State's obligations under EU law. The court also stated that Arts 1 and 5 of the Constitution gave the Irish State full sovereignty in relation to foreign affairs.

In this case Finlay CJ stated that if the new EU Treaty altered the original aims and objectives of the European Communities there would be a need for an Irish referendum. If the Treaty did not alter the objectives and aims of the European Communities a referendum would not be needed.

Chapter 6

Preliminary Rulings

INTRODUCTION

[6.01] Article 267 TFEU (ex Art 234 TEC) contains the provisions for the preliminary reference procedure. The provisions are as follows:

> 'The Court of Justice of the European Union shall have jurisdiction to give preliminary rulings concerning:
>
> (a)   the interpretation of the Treaties;
>
> (b)   the validity and interpretation of acts of the institutions, bodies, offices or agencies of the Union;
>
> Where such a question is raised before any court or tribunal of a Member State, that court or tribunal may, if it considers that a decision on the question is necessary to enable it to give judgment, request the Court to give a ruling thereon.
>
> Where any such question is raised in a case pending before a court or tribunal of a Member State against whose decisions there is no judicial remedy under national law, that court or tribunal shall bring the matter before the Court.
>
> If such a question is raised in a case pending before a court or tribunal of a Member State with regard to a person in custody, the Court of Justice of the European Union shall act with the minimum of delay.'

When a national court is applying European Union law an issue may arise in relation to the interpretation or validity of the piece of law in question. If this occurs the national court may use the preliminary reference procedure to ask the Court of Justice of the European Union a question in relation to the piece of European Union law.

The preliminary reference procedure allows the national court to send a preliminary reference to the Court of Justice comprising the question on European Union law and an outline of the facts and legal issues arising in the case. The national court will wait for an answer from the Court of Justice and it will then decide the case in line with the correct application of European Union law.

The Court of Justice will only give a preliminary ruling on the interpretation or validity of European Union law. The Court of Justice has no role in deciding what should be the final outcome of the matter before the national court. The preliminary reference procedure is not an appeals procedure.

Article 267 TFEU provides for the integration of European Union law into the national legal systems of the Member States. The procedure promotes uniform interpretation and application of European Union law and it also ensures legal certainty.

Article 267 TFEU has also played a significant role in the development of European Union law. The preliminary reference procedure has provided the Court of Justice with a mechanism to develop fundamental constitutional principles such as supremacy and direct effect. For example the principle of direct effect was established as a result of a reference made by a Dutch court in the case of *Van Gend en Loos v Administratie der Balastingen* (Case C–26/62), [1963] ECR 1.

'A COURT OR TRIBUNAL' PURSUANT TO ART 267 TFEU

[6.02] Article 267 TFEU states that any court or tribunal of a Member State may seek a preliminary ruling. What constitutes 'a court or tribunal' for the purpose of Art 267 TFEU is a matter of European Union law. How the body is categorised under national law is not conclusive as to how it will be categorised under European Union law. As a result the Court of Justice has provided guidance through its case law on what constitutes a 'court or tribunal'.

To date the Court of Justice has developed a broad definition of 'court or tribunal'. In *Broeckmeulen v Huisarts Registratie Commissie* (Case C–246/80), [1981] ECR 2311 the court had to decide if an appeals committee for the Dutch medical professional body was a court or tribunal for the purposes of Art 267 TFEU. Despite the fact that Dutch law did not recognise the appeals committee as a court or tribunal, the European court ruled that the appeals committee was a court or tribunal for the purposes of European Union law. The reason for the court's decision was that the appeals committee operated with the consent and cooperation of the public authorities and that it delivered final decisions after an adversarial procedure from which there was no right of appeal to the ordinary courts.

[6.03] In the case of *Dorsch Consult Ingenieurgesellschaft v Bundesbaugesellschaft* (Case C–54/96), [1997] ECR I–4961 the court set out the criteria to be applied when considering whether a body is a 'court or tribunal'. The court will take account of the following factors:

- whether the body is established by law;

- whether it is permanent;

- whether its jurisdiction is compulsory;

- whether its procedure is *inter partes* (court proceedings involving two sides);

- whether it applies rules of law; and

- whether it is independent.

These factors were reaffirmed in the case of *De Coster v Collège des bourgmestre et échevins de Watermael-Boitsfort* (Case C–17/00), [2001] ECR I–9445.

Arbitrators are not generally recognised as a 'court or tribunal'. In *Nordsee Deutsche Hochseefischerei Gmbh v Reederei Mond Hochseefischerei Nordstern AG & Co* (Case C–102/81), [1982] ECR 1095 the parties entered into a private agreement whereby in the event of a dispute, they would go to an arbitrator instead of going to court. The Court of Justice ruled that the arbitrator was not a 'court or tribunal'. The court provided two reasons for this decision. First, an arbitrator would not be considered a 'court or tribunal' when the parties were not obliged to refer the dispute to an arbitrator. Secondly, the public authorities were not involved in the decision to refer the dispute to arbitration and the public authorities were not automatically called upon to intervene in the arbitration.

Irish examples of what constitutes a 'court or tribunal' include, the courts which form part of the Irish legal system, the Employment Appeals Tribunal, An Bord Pleanála and the Labour Court.

THE DISCRETION TO MAKE A PRELIMINARY REFERENCE

[6.04] National courts have a discretion to refer questions under Art 267(2) TFEU. When a question relating to European Union law is raised before any court or tribunal of a Member State, the court or tribunal may request the Court of Justice to give a preliminary ruling once it considers that a decision on the question is necessary to enable it to give judgment. When Article 267(2) TFEU applies, a national court cannot be compelled to make a reference either by the Court of Justice or the parties. If the national court exercises its discretion to make a reference there are a number of factors to be considered:

- There must be a genuine dispute and the question should not be hypothetical.

- The question must be relevant to the dispute before the national court.

- The reference should contain sufficient factual and legal information.

- Does a precedent already exist or does the *acte clair* doctrine apply? If so there may not be a need to make a preliminary reference (the *acte clair* doctrine will be explained later in this chapter).

- Does the question challenge the validity of European Union Law? If so, the national court must make a preliminary reference as national courts do not have the power to declare European Union law invalid.

THE DUTY TO MAKE A PRELIMINARY REFERENCE

[6.05] The duty to refer arises when the national court in question is a court of final instance. Therefore, if there is no right of appeal from that court, the national court is obliged and has a duty to make a preliminary reference. This provision is contained in Art 267(3) TFEU.

In Ireland, the Supreme Court is clearly a court of final instance and, as such, it is obliged to make a preliminary reference if it is necessary to enable it to give judgment. However, deciding what constitutes a court of final instance is not always straightforward. For example, some cases might never reach the Supreme Court because the right of appeal is exhausted in the High Court. Two theories emerged to address this problem:

Abstract Theory

[6.06] The abstract theory suggests that only courts which occupy the highest position in the national legal system are obliged to make preliminary references.

Concrete Theory

[6.07] The concrete theory suggests that a court of last instance is a court from which there is no right of appeal in a particular case. According to the concrete theory a court of final instance is determined on a case-by-case basis.

It appears from the case law of the Court of Justice that the preferred approach is the concrete theory. In *Costa v ENEL* (Case C–6/64), [1964] ECR 585 a case was heard before the Italian magistrates' court but it concerned such a small amount of money that there was no right of appeal to a higher national court. The Court of Justice ruled that national courts against whose decisions there is no judicial remedy must refer the matter to the Court of Justice.

EXCEPTIONS TO THE DUTY TO REFER

[6.08] There are situations when even a court of final instance does not need to make a preliminary reference. These exceptions were created and developed by the Court of Justice.

In *Da Costa en Schaake NV v Nederlandse Belastingadministratie* (Case C–28–30/62), [1963] ECR 31 the facts and the questions of interpretation were materially identical to those raised in the earlier decision of *Van Gend en Loos* (Case C–26/62), [1963] ECR 1. The Court of Justice stated that Art 177 (now Art 267(3) TFEU) unreservedly requires courts or tribunals of final instance to refer every question of interpretation raised before them. However, the Court went on to say that despite this requirement, 'the authority of an interpretation under Art 177 (now Art 267(3) TFEU) already given by the Court may deprive the obligation of its purpose and thus empty it of its substance'. Therefore, a previous ruling of an identical nature removes the obligation to refer. A court or tribunal of a Member State could still refer a question if there were new factors or arguments but if this was not the case the Court would simply refer the national court to its previous ruling.

The Court developed this exception further in *CILFIT Srl v Ministero della Sanita* (Case C–283/81), [1982] ECR 3415 by stating that if there was a previous ruling on the same point of law there would be no obligation to refer even if the facts were not strictly identical. This restatement of the Court's decision in *Da Costa* was intended to clarify the scope of the exception.

[6.09] The court's decision in *CILFIT* went on to examine two further exceptions. The second exception arises when there is no question of European Union law. In *CILFIT* the Italian Ministry of Health argued that the answer to the question on European Union law was so obvious it ruled out the need for a reference. The claimants argued that since a question of European Union law had been raised before a court of final instance the court could not escape its obligation to seek a preliminary ruling. The court stated that a court of final instance has a discretion to ascertain if a decision on a question is necessary to enable it to give judgment. Consequently, a court of final instance has no obligation to refer if the question on European Union law is irrelevant and will not affect the outcome of the case.

The third exception established in *CILFIT* is the 'acte clair' doctrine. This phrase means that the law is clear or not in need of interpretation. The 'acte clair' doctrine applies to situations where 'the correct application of community law is so obvious as to leave no scope for any reasonable doubt'. If the doctrine applies to the piece of European Union law at issue in a particular case then there is no need for the national court to seek a preliminary ruling.

In order to help national courts in applying the 'acte clair' doctrine the court provided guidelines in *CILFIT*:

- The national court must be convinced that the matter is equally obvious to the courts of other Member States and to the Court of Justice.

- European Union law is drafted in several different languages and the national court should compare these different languages in order to eliminate any possibility of doubt and to reach the most accurate interpretation.

- The national court should note that legal terminology in European Union law is unique and it may not have the same meaning as it does in national law.

- The national court should interpret European Union law in context and in light of the objectives of the treaties.

The 'acte clair' doctrine allows national courts to interpret the provisions of European Union law. However, an incorrect interpretation of the doctrine can potentially carry risks. In *Köbler v Austria* (Case C–224/01), [2003] ECR I–10239 the court ruled that if it was manifestly apparent that a national court had not complied with its obligations under Art 234(3) TEU (now Art 267(3) TFEU) then state liability in damages would arise.

Summary of the situations where there is an exception to the duty to refer

1. Where the Court of Justice has previously provided an authority on the point at issue.

2. Where no question of European Union law arises.

3. Where the 'acte clair' doctrine applies.

CIRCUMSTANCES WHEN COURT OF JUSTICE WILL NOT ENTERTAIN REFERENCE

[6.10] The Court of Justice will declare a reference inadmissible in a number of situations. This can occur even if a national court is complying with its obligation to make a reference. The Court of Justice will refuse jurisdiction where there is no genuine dispute between the parties, where the question is irrelevant to the dispute between the parties, and where there is insufficient factual or legal information.

(a)   Where there is no genuine dispute between the parties

This situation was examined in *Foglia v Novello (No 1)* (Case C–104/79), [1980] ECR 745 and *Foglia v Novello (No 2)* (Case C–244/80), [1981] ECR 3045. The facts of the case had been contrived by the parties in order to challenge French tax law in an Italian court. The Court of Justice refused to entertain the reference because there was no genuine dispute between the parties. The Italian court made a further reference in *Foglia (No 2)* questioning the court's refusal of jurisdiction. The court again refused jurisdiction and stated that it did not have a duty to deliver advisory opinions on general or hypothetical questions.

(b)   Where the question is irrelevant to the dispute between the parties.

In *Meilicke v ADV/ORGA FA Meyer AG (Case C–83/91),* [1992] ECR I–4871 the German courts referred a question asking if the theory of disguised non-cash subscriptions was compatible with the Second Banking Directive. The court refused to give a ruling because there was no evidence to show that the issue of non-cash subscriptions was relevant to the case before the German court.

(c)   Where there is insufficient factual or legal information.

In *Telemarsicabruzzo SpA v Circostel* (Case C–320–322/90), [1993] ECR I–393 an Italian court referred questions asking if the national provisions on the distribution of TV frequencies was compatible with EC competition law. The Italian court did not provide sufficient factual information to allow the ECJ to address the questions. The court was unable to interpret the competition rules at issue because it was not aware of the facts underlying the main proceedings.

Chapter 7

Direct Effect

INTRODUCTION

[7.01] There is no express reference to direct effect in the European Treaties and the concept of direct effect was developed by the Court of Justice of the European Union through its case law. Direct effect allows a provision of EU law to be applied in national courts. If a provision has direct effect an individual can enforce that provision before the national courts.

CONDITIONS FOR DIRECT EFFECT

[7.02] The concept of direct effect was established in *Van Gend en Loos* (Case C–26/62), [1963] ECR 1. In this case the court was asked whether a company could rely on a provision of the EC Treaty. The court held that the EC Treaty had established a new legal order which was capable of creating rights for individuals and these rights could be enforced in national courts.

However, in order for a provision to have direct effect three conditions must be met:

1. the provision must be clear and precise;
2. the provision must be unconditional; and
3. the provision must not require any further action by a member state for enactment.

When all three conditions are met the provision has direct effect.

DIRECT EFFECT OF PRIMARY AND SECONDARY LEGISLATION

[7.03] Treaty provisions and international agreements concluded by the EU are sources of primary law and they both have direct effect.

Regulations and decisions are sources of secondary legislation. The court has concluded that both regulations and decisions have direct effect.

DIRECT EFFECT OF DIRECTIVES

[7.04] Another source of secondary legislation is the directive. Whether or not a directive was capable of having direct effect required careful analysis and development by the Court of Justice. The directive is a very important legal instrument and it plays a vital role in the European legal framework. The purpose of a directive is to reconcile two objectives. These objectives are:

1.   establishing uniformity within Union law; and

2.   respecting the diversity of national legal traditions.

The primary aim of a directive is harmonisation that allows the same legal conditions to exist in all Member States. However this aim is not always easily achieved.

According to Art 288 TFEU directives are binding as to the result to be achieved and the Member States have a choice in relation to the form and methods used to achieve the result. Directives could not have direct effect on foot of these criteria. However the Court of Justice developed the possibility of directives having direct effect through its decisions.

[7.05] In *Van Duyn v Home Office* (C–Case 41/74), [1974] ECR 1337 the court concluded that directives are capable of generating directly effective rights. The court stated that it would be incompatible with the binding effect attributed to a directive to exclude individuals from enforcing the rights created by the directive in their national courts. The court went on to say that the rights created by a directive would be weakened if individuals were prevented from relying on the rights before their national courts and if the national courts were prevented from taking the rights into consideration.

In *Ratti* (Case 148/78), [1979] ECR 1629 the court stated that in order for a directive to have direct effect the time frame prescribed for transposing the directive must have passed. The court went on to say that a Member State's obligation to transpose a directive only becomes absolute when the time limit for transposing the directive has expired.

VERTICAL AND HORIZONTAL DIRECT EFFECT

[7.06] Vertical effect means that an individual can enforce a provision against a Member State before a national court.

Horizontal effect means that an individual can enforce a provision against another individual before a national court.

- Treaties can be both vertically and horizontally effective.

- Regulations can be both vertically and horizontally effective.

- Directives can only be vertically effective.

Vertical Direct Effect of Directives

[7.07] Directives are expressly addressed to the Member States only and directives do not confer rights or impose obligations on Union citizens. Once a Member State transposes a directive into national law the Union citizen is then granted rights and obligations on foot of the piece of implemented national legislation.

A union citizen may suffer disadvantages when a Member State does not transpose a directive or they may also suffer disadvantages if a directive is transposed incorrectly. As a result a Union citizen will not enjoy the benefits of the objectives sought to be achieved by the European Union.

The Court of Justice has refused to tolerate such disadvantages for citizens. If a Union citizen is suffering a disadvantage because a directive has not been transposed by a Member State then the citizen can plead vertical direct effect of the directive's objectives in the national court. The justification for vertical direct effect is that it would be unfair to allow a Member State to benefit and to escape its duties as a result of failure to transpose a directive.

[7.08] The following conditions must be present in order for the citizen to establish vertical direct effect.

- The provision must give clearly identifiable rights to individuals.

- The timeframe for transposing the directive must have expired.

- The provision can only be enforced vertically against a Member State.

Vertical direct effect is a means of monitoring and keeping Member States in check. Directives only have vertical direct effect and a citizen can never rely on a directive against another individual (horizontal direct effect).

The Court of Justice has refused to extend the application of horizontal direct effect to directives. The rationale for this is that an individual cannot be held liable for the failure of a Member State to meet its obligations under EU Law.

The Court made it clear in *Marshall v Southampton Health and South West Area Health Authority* (Case C–152/84), [1986] ECR 723 that there was no possibility of extending horizontal direct effect to directives. The claimant had been employed by the Southampton Health Authority and when she reached the age of 62 she was dismissed due to the fact that she had reached the authority's retirement age for females. She attempted to challenge her employer's compulsory retirement policy by relying on the Equal Treatment Directive 76/206 and she claimed that the retirement policy was discriminatory. The claimant's employer was deemed to be a part of the state and as a result the claimant was successful with her vertical action. Even though the claimant's action was vertical the court took the opportunity to comment on horizontal direct effect and stated that a directive can only be relied on vertically and they were not capable of creating rights through horizontal direct effect.

[7.09] Due to the fact that directives can only give rise to vertical direct effect the definition of 'the state' has been the focus of subsequent case law and analysis. The court has applied a broad interpretation as to what is considered 'the state' or 'an emanation of the State'.

In *Foster v British Gas* (Case 188/89), [1990] ECR 1–3313 the court considered the meaning of 'emanation of the State'. The claimant was employed by British Gas and the employers had in place different retirement ages for men and women. The claimant attempted to rely on the Equal Treatment Directive 76/207 in order to challenge the different compulsory retirement ages for men and women. The Court of Justice provided a definition for what constitutes an emanation of the State. It is 'a body, whatever its legal form, which has been made responsible, pursuant to a measure adopted by the State, for providing a public service under the control of the state and has for that purpose special powers beyond those which result from the normal rules applicable in relations between individuals'. If a body comes within this definition it is an emanation of the state and it is possible to rely on a directive against such a body.

Therefore the three conditions prescribed by the court are;

1. The body must be providing a public service.

2. The public service must be under the control of the state.

3. The body must have special powers in excess of those that apply between individuals

INDIRECT EFFECT

[7.10] The courts refusal to extend horizontal direct effect to directives has been addressed by the court through the creation of indirect effect.

In *Van Colson and Kamman v Land Nordrhein-Westfalen* (Case 14/ 83), [1984] ECR 1891 the claimants sought to rely on the equal treatment directive however the court held that the directive did not have direct effect. Despite this finding the court held that Member States are under an obligation pursuant to Art 4 TFEU to take all appropriate measures to fulfil their obligations under EU law. This duty is extends to the national courts who must interpret national law with reference to the purpose and wording of the directive and EU law.

In *Marleasing v La Comercial Internacional de Alimentacion SA* (Case 106/89), the court developed the principle of indirect effect further and stated that it applies irrespective of when the national law is adopted.

STATE LIABILITY

[7.11] If an individual fails to obtain a remedy through direct or indirect effect it is possible to seek a remedy through state liability. The principle of state liability allows individuals who have suffered a loss as a result of a breach of EU Law to obtain damages from the member state responsible for the breach. Students should note that state liability arises mainly in relation to directives but it can also arise in other areas.

In *Francovich and Bonifaci v Republic of Italy (Case 9/90)*, [1991] ECR 1–5357 the court developed the principle of state liability. In this case the claimants had been made redundant and they were attempting to obtain payment arrears from their bankrupt employer. They were seeking to rely on Council Directive 80/897/EEC however they were unable to rely on the directive either directly or indirectly. The court held that Italy had failed to fulfil its Treaty obligations by not implementing Council Directive 80/897/EEC. On foot of the finding the claimants were able to recover damages against the state for the loss suffered due to the state's failure to transpose the directive.

[7.12] The right to damages is not absolute and it is subject to certain conditions. The court held that where a Member State fails to implement a directive the right to damages depends on the following three conditions being met:

1. the result required by the directive includes the granting of rights to individuals;

2. the content of those rights must be identifiable from the directive; and

3. a causal link must exist between the member state's breach and the damage suffered by the individual.

The decision in *Francovich* failed to address what would happen if a Member State transposed a directive incorrectly or only partially. In this regard subsequent case law from the court has provided much needed clarification.

[7.13] In joined cases *Brasserie du Pêcheur SA v Federal Republic of Germany and R v Secretary of State for Transport, ex p Factortame Ltd and Others* (Cases C–46/93 and C–48/93), [1996] ECR I–1029 the court elaborated on the criteria for liability in cases involving a breach other than non-transposition.

The court held that the right to damages depends on the nature of the breach. The following conditions for obtaining damages were held to apply when a member state enjoys a wide discretion under EU Law.

1. The rule of law infringed must be intended to confer rights on individuals.

2. The breach must be sufficiently serious.

3. There must be a causal link between the breach of the obligation by the member state and the damage sustained by the injured parties.

The test for a 'sufficiently serious' breach is whether the member state has manifestly and gravely disregarded the limits on its discretion.

The court may take a number of factors into account during its assessment of 'sufficiently serious'. These factors include:

- The clarity and precision of the rule breached;

- The measure of discretion left by that rule to the national or Community authorities Whether the infringement and the damage caused was intentional or involuntary;

- Whether any error of law was excusable or inexcusable;

- The fact that the position taken by a Community institution may have contributed towards the omission; and

- The adoption or retention of national measures or practices contrary to Community law.

[7.14] The principle of state liability was developed further in *Köbler v Austria* (Case C–224/01), [2003] ECR I–10239. In this case the court extended state liability to a decision of a national court of last instance. The claimant was a university professor who was refused a pay increment because he did not meet Austrian university requirements. He claimed that there was a breach of the free movement provisions due to this requirement and further that the national court had wrongly interpreted EU law.

The Court of Justice found that the national court's interpretation of EU law was not correct and that the national court had failed to re-refer a preliminary question to the court. The court went on to say that an incorrect interpretation of EU law by a court of final instance is grounds for state liability. However in the case of *Köbler* the court found that the breach was not sufficiently serious.

THE DIRECT EFFECT OF EU LAW IN IRELAND

[7.15] European Union law becomes part of Irish law without incorporation by the Oireachtas and this is an exception to the provisions of Article 15.2.1° of the Irish Constitution that provides only the Oireachtas may make laws for the Irish State.

As a result of Art 29 of the Irish Constitution, European Union law is not viewed in the same way as international law and EU law and international law are treated completely differently. EU law is automatically incorporated into Irish law and as such it has direct applicability. EU law can also have direct effect in Ireland and this allows Irish individuals to rely on EU law in Irish courts even though the Oireachtas has not incorporated the specific EU law measure. The direct effect of EU laws in Ireland is established and allowed by Art 29 of the Irish Constitution and the provisions of the Constitution are built upon by national legislation.

Despite these provisions there are situations when a piece of EU legislation will require the Member States to take measures in order to implement the legislation into national law. Directives are an example of a piece of EU legislation where a Member State must implement the provisions of the directive into national law. The Member States will always be able to choose how the purpose of the directive is to be achieved. In order for the directive to become a piece of Irish law, it must be incorporated into national law by the Irish State. Directives are different to regulations as EU regulations do not require incorporation.

The main question for Ireland in this situation has been how can EU laws be implemented by delegated legislation? The main difficulty has been whether or not implementation can occur through statutory instrument or whether it must be through an Act of the Oireachtas. Ireland has enacted national legislation to address these shortcomings (see further **Ch 5** on Supremacy).

Chapter 8

Enforcement of EU Law

INTRODUCTION

[8.01] Member States have a duty to fulfil their obligations under EU law. Articles 258–260 TFEU contain the provisions on enforcement of EU law. If a Member State breaches EU law enforcement proceedings can be brought by either the Commission or another Member State directly in the Court of Justice.

Article 258 TFEU provides for actions to be brought against Member States by the Commission. Article 259 TFEU provides for actions to be brought against a Member State by another Member State. Article 260 TFEU works in conjunction with these two provisions by requiring Member States to comply with the Court's decision.

The enforcement of EU law is divided between public and private enforcement. As a result a system of 'dual enforcement' operates within the EU. Direct actions in the Court of Justice brought by the Commission or a Member State are referred to as the public enforcement of EU law. Direct effect, indirect effect and state liability form part of the private enforcement of EU law.

ARTICLE 258 TFEU

[8.02] The treaty provisions under Art 258 TFEU provide the following:

> 'If the Commission considers that a Member State has failed to fulfil an obligation under the Treaties, it shall deliver a reasoned opinion on the matter after giving the State concerned the opportunity to submit its observations.
>
> If the State concerned does not comply with the opinion within the period laid down by the Commission, the latter

may bring the matter before the Court of Justice of the
European Union.'

Enforcement actions brought by the Commission against a Member
State are taken pursuant to Art 258 TFEU.

In *Starfruit v Commission* (Case 247/87), [1989] ECR 291, Starfruit
made a complaint to the Commission stating that the French banana
market was organised in a manner that was contrary to EU law and
as a result France was in breach of its EU obligations. The
Commission used its discretion and it did not pursue the complaint
brought by Starfruit. However, Starfruit then brought proceedings
against the Commission for its failure to commence proceedings
against France. The Court of Justice held that the Commission does
not have a duty to commence proceedings, rather it has a discretion
to commence proceedings. Individuals cannot force the Commission
to commence proceedings.

ARTICLE 258 TFEU PROCEDURE

[8.03] If the Commission decides to bring proceeding against a
Member State for breaches of EU law a certain procedure must be
followed. The procedure to be followed is contained in Art 258
TFEU and it incorporates a number of required elements.

The procedure under Art 258 is divided into two stages,

1.   the administrative stage; and

2.   the judicial stage.

The administrative process begins with the Commission making
informal contact with the Member State. If the response from the
Member State is not adequate the Commission can then commence
the formal procedure. The first step of the formal administrative
stage is a letter of formal notice. The Commission sends a letter to
the Member State outlining the reasons for suspecting an
infringement of EU law has occurred. The Member State is then
given time to respond to this letter of formal notice. At this point the

Member State and the Commission often engage in negotiations and they attempt to resolve the matter. If a resolution is not reached the Commission then moves on to the next stage. The next step in the administrative stage is a recent opinion from the Commission. The reasoned opinion sets out the exact grounds of the complaint. The reasoned opinion also provides the Member State with a time limit for a responding. A Member State is expected to end the infringement within the time limit specified. However if the time limit expires and the infringement has not ceased the next phase of the procedure begins.

[8.04] The next phase of the procedure is the judicial stage. During the judicial stage the matter is referred to the Court of Justice and the court is asked to provide a ruling on the matter. At this point only the contents of the reasoned opinion can be relied upon by the Commission. Interested Member States may intervene in the proceedings before the Court of Justice, however individuals cannot.

A Member State may raise a number of defences during the proceedings before the Court of Justice. The main defences that have been put forward by Member States are as follows:

1. Force majeure (*Commission v Italy* (Case 101/84))

2. Reciprocity (breach by another Member State allows the defaulting Member State to withdraw from its treaty obligation)

3. Practical difficulties (*'Tachographs' case* (Case 128/78))

Member States have not been successful when they raise defences before the Court of Justice of the European Union. The most likely defence to succeed is *force majeure. Force majeure* relates to unforeseeable circumstances which are out of the control of the person who is committing the infringement.

[8.05]

Article 258 TFEU Procedure

- Informal contact with Member State.

Administrative stage

- Letter of Formal Notice;
- Reasoned Opinion.

Judicial Stage

- Referral to the Court of Justice;
- Ruling from the Court of Justice;
- Financial penalty (Art 260 TFEU).

INTERIM MEASURES

[8.06] The process can take a number of months and it may be necessary to stop a particular action during this time frame. In order to address this issue Arts 278 and 279 TFEU provide for suspension orders and interim orders.

ARTICLE 259 TFEU

[8.07] It is also possible for a Member State to bring an action against another Member State when the Member State has failed to fulfil its EU obligations. This process begins with a complaint being made before the Commission. Both sides are then asked to give submissions and the Commission delivers a reasoned opinion and seeks a settlement. It is possible for the Commission to take over the action. Article 259 actions do not happen very often, and this is due to the fact that Member States prefer, for political reasons, to ask the Commission to act under Art 258.

ARTICLE 260 TFEU

[8.08] Article 260 TFEU requires Member States to comply with the court's decision and pursuant to Art 260 TFEU if a Member State has not taken the necessary measures to comply with a decision, the Commission may refer the matter to the Court of Justice.

According to Article 260 TFEU, the Commission can recommend an appropriate lump sum or penalty payment. However, the Court of Justice is not bound to follow this recommendation. Calculation of the penalty payment is based on a method that takes account of the seriousness of the infringement, having regard to the importance of the rules breached and the impact of the infringement on general and particular interests, its duration and the Member State's ability to pay, with a view to ensuring that the penalty itself has a deterrent effect.

There is no upper limit on the penalty payment and the penalty payment can include a dual financial penalty. The penalty payment can incorporate a lump sum payment for the infringement and a penalty payment in respect of each day that the Member State fails to comply with the judgment.

The Lisbon Treaty introduced a number of changes to the enforcement procedure. Article 260(2) TFEU states:

> 'If the Commission considers that the Member State concerned has not taken the necessary measures to comply with the judgment of the Court, it may bring the case before the Court after giving that State the opportunity to submit its observations. It shall specify the amount of the lump sum or penalty payment to be paid by the Member State concerned which it considers appropriate in the circumstances.

> If the Court finds that the Member State concerned has not complied with its judgment it may impose a lump sum or penalty payment on it.

> This procedure shall be without prejudice to Art 259.'

The Commission is no longer obliged to wait for a State to submit observations or to issue a reasoned opinion before bringing the matter to court and the process is expedited as a result.

Article 260(3) TFEU provides the following:

> 'When the Commission brings a case before the Court pursuant to Article 258 on the grounds that the Member State concerned has failed to fulfil its obligation to notify

measures transposing a directive adopted under a legislative procedure, it may, when it deems appropriate, specify the amount of the lump sum or penalty payment to be paid by the Member State concerned which it considers appropriate in the circumstances.

If the Court finds that there is an infringement it may impose a lump sum or penalty payment on the Member State concerned not exceeding the amount specified by the Commission. The payment obligation shall take effect on the date set by the Court in its judgment.'

The key amending features of this provision are that the court may not impose a lump sum or a penalty payment on a Member State that exceeds the amount specified by the Commission and the court will impose the fine at a date specified in its judgment.

The court applied Art 228 EC (now Art 260 TFEU) in *Commission v France* (Case 304/02) and imposed both a lump sum and a penalty payment. The reason for this decision stemmed from *Commission v France* (Case C–64/88) where France failed to comply with the court's judgment.

In *Commission v France* (Case C–121/07) the court ordered France to pay only a lump sum of €10 million for failing to comply with the court's 2004 judgment. The reason for the 2004 judgment was that France had failed to transpose a directive into national law. France then transposed the directive in 2008 and as a result the court held there was no need for a penalty payment. However, as the breach had still occurred and given the seriousness and length of time for which it had occurred, the lump sum fine was still imposed.

Chapter 9

Judicial Review

INTRODUCTION

[9.01] Article 263 TFEU (ex Art 230 TEC) outlines the procedure whereby acts adopted by the EU institutions can be challenged in EU courts. The acts can be challenged by Member States, EU institutions and individuals. A challenge is brought before the Court of Justice of the European Union and the applicant seeks a review of legality of the act. If an act is successfully challenged the act will be annulled. A challenge brought in this way is called a direct action.

The wording of Art 263 TFEU is as follows:

ARTICLE 263 TFEU

(EX ARTICLE 230 TEC)

'The Court of Justice of the European Union shall review the legality of legislative acts, of acts of the Council, of the Commission and of the European Central Bank, other than recommendations and opinions, and of acts of the European Parliament and of the European Council intended to produce legal effects vis-à-vis third parties. It shall also review the legality of acts of bodies, offices or agencies of the Union intended to produce legal effects vis-à-vis third parties.

It shall for this purpose have jurisdiction in actions brought by a Member State, the European Parliament, the Council or the Commission on grounds of lack of competence, infringement of an essential procedural requirement, infringement of the Treaties or of any rule of law relating to their application, or misuse of powers.

The Court shall have jurisdiction under the same conditions in actions brought by the Court of Auditors, by the European

Central Bank and by the Committee of the Regions for the purpose of protecting their prerogatives.

Any natural or legal person may, under the conditions laid down in the first and second paragraphs, institute proceedings against an act addressed to that person or which is of direct and individual concern to them, and against a regulatory act which is of direct concern to them and does not entail implementing measures.

Acts setting up bodies, offices and agencies of the Union may lay down specific conditions and arrangements concerning actions brought by natural or legal persons against acts of these bodies, offices or agencies intended to produce legal effects in relation to them.

The proceedings provided for in this Article shall be instituted within two months of the publication of the measure, or of its notification to the plaintiff, or, in the absence thereof, of the day on which it came to the knowledge of the latter, as the case may be.'

An EU act may be challenged for any of the following reasons:

- lack of competence;

- infringement of an essential procedural requirement;

- infringement of the Treaties or of any rule of law relating to their application; and

- misuse of powers.

[9.02] Article 263 TFEU provides a description of the type of act/ piece of legislation that may be challenged.

Recommendations and opinions are not acts for the purpose of a challenge under Art 263 TFEU. The acts which can be challenged are those that produce legal effects vis-à-vis third parties.

It is clear that regulations, directives and decisions fall within the scope of reviewable acts, however other acts can be subject to review. In *Commission v Council* (Case 22/70), [1971] ECR 263 it was held that all measures adopted by the institutions which are intended to have legal force are open to review.

The review of legality is subject to a time limit and an action must be commenced 'within two months of the publication of the measure, or of its notification to the plaintiff, or, in the absence thereof, of the day on which it came to the knowledge of the latter'.

Direct actions to challenge an act adopted by the EU institutions can be brought by different types of applicants. The Member States, the Council, the Commission and the Parliament are classified as privileged applicants. The Court of Auditors, the European Central Bank and the Committee of the Regions are classified as semi-privileged applicants. Natural and legal persons which include individuals and companies are classified as non-privileged applicants.

Privileged applicants have an automatic right of access to the court and semi-privileged applicants have access to the court 'for the purpose of protecting their prerogatives'. Non-privileged applicants have a restricted right of access to the court.

LOCUS STANDI REQUIREMENTS FOR NON-PRIVILEGED APPLICANTS

[9.03] *Locus standi* is the right that an individual has to be heard in court. In some circumstances it is necessary for the applicant to establish that they have the right to be heard before the court case can commence. The *locus standi* requirements will differ depending on the level of the court and due to the nature of the matter being challenged. If the court has *locus standi* requirements the applicant must make a *locus standi* application. The *locus standi* application is made before the court case starts and if the applicant is successful with the *locus standi* application the court case can commence. A successful *locus standi* application does not mean that the outcome of the case will be successful, it merely allowing an individual to make their case in court. If the individual cannot establish *locus* *standi* the case will be dismissed and the merits of the argument will not be considered.

Article 263 TFEU states that a natural or legal person may 'institute proceedings against an act addressed to that person or which is of direct and individual concern to them, and against a regulatory act which is of direct concern to them and does not entail implementing measures'.

There are three types of EU act which a non-privileged applicant has *locus standi* to challenge. The acts open to challenge are as follows:

1. an act which is addressed to the non-privileged applicant;

2. an act addressed to another person but which is of direct and individual concern to the non-privileged applicant;

3. a regulatory act which is of direct concern to the non-privileged applicant and which does not entail implementing measures.

A REGULATORY ACT WHICH IS OF DIRECT CONCERN

[9.04] Article 263 TFEU represents a reformulation of the former Art 230 EC. The Lisbon Treaty introduced new wording which allows non-privileged applicants to challenge a regulatory act which is of direct concern to them and which does not entail implementing measures.

The changes allow non-privileged applicants to challenge regulatory acts without having to prove individual concern. However, the expression 'a regulatory act' is not defined in the treaties and the meaning will have to be interpreted by the Court of Justice. How the Court decides to interpret the expression will have a bearing on the standing of non-privileged applicants. Until further clarification is provided by the court the reform for non-privileged applicants appears to be limited.

DIRECT AND INDIVIDUAL CONCERN

[9.05] When an act is addressed to a non-privileged applicant access to the court is not problematic. In these circumstances an act can be challenged once the time limit is adhered to.

However, in order to successfully challenge an act addressed to another person a non-privileged applicant must show 'direct and individual concern'. The Court of Justice has interpreted 'direct and individual concern' strictly and as a result, it is very difficult for non-privileged applicants to challenge an EU act and to obtain a review of legality.

Direct Concern

[9.06] In order to satisfy the 'direct concern' requirements a non-privileged applicant must show:

1. that the act directly affects their legal situation; and

2. that no discretion is given to a Member State in the implementation of the act.

In order for an act to directly affect a non-privileged applicant's legal situation there must be a causal link between the damage suffered by the applicant and the offending act.

However, if a Member State is given a discretion in relation to the implementation of the act the non-privileged applicant is affected by the implementation and not the act. When a Member State has a discretion a causal link will not be established.

In *Société Louis Dreyfus & Cie v Commission* (Case 386/96P), [1998] ECR I–2309 para 43 the Court of Justice held that the act being challenged

'Must directly affect the legal situation of the individual and leave no discretion to the addressees of that measure who are entrusted with the task of implementing it, such implementation being purely automatic and resulting from

Community rules without the application of other intermediate rules'.

In *Municipality of Differdange v Commission* (Case 222/83), steel producers were granted aid on foot of a decision addressed to Luxembourg. The applicant sought to have the decision annulled on the basis that there would be a reduction in local tax revenue. However, the Court did not find in favour of the applicant. The decision left a discretion to the national authorities in terms of implementation and it was this discretion that affected the applicant not the decision.

Individual Concern

[9.07] The 'individual concern' requirement has been interpreted in a restrictive manner by the Court of Justice and as a result it has caused a great deal of difficulty for non-privileged applicants who wish to challenge an act or piece of legislation. The individual concern requirement is one of the most difficult hurdles for non-privileged applicants to overcome in terms of *locus standi*.

The interpretation of 'individual concern' is outlined in *Plaumann & Co v Commission* (Case 25/62), [1963] ECR 95 in this case the Court of Justice held that:

> 'Persons other than those to whom a decision is addressed may only claim to be individually concerned if that decision affects them by reason of certain attributes which are peculiar to them or by reason of the circumstances in which they are differentiated from all other persons and by virtue of these factors distinguishes them individually just as in the case of the person addressed.'

In the *Plaumann* the Commission addressed a decision to the German government and the content of the decision concerned an import tax on clementines.

Plaumann was a clementine importer and he sought to challenge this decision by claiming 'direct and individual concern'. However, the court found that Plaumann was not 'individually concerned' and stated that individual concern could only be established by applicants 'by reason of certain attributes which are peculiar to them or by reason of circumstances in which they are differentiated from all other persons'.

Plaumann was not individually concerned despite being adversely affected by the decision. The reason for this was that Plaumann by being involved in the clementine business was part of an open class of individuals involved in that business and as such he was not individually concerned.

[9.08] An open class of individuals is a group containing an unascertainable number of individuals at the time the act is passed. A closed class of individuals is a group containing a fixed and ascertainable number of individuals at the time the act is passed.

Despite the difficulties in proving individual concern non-privileged applicants have been successful in establishing 'individual concern' when they are part of a closed class of individuals.

In *Piraiki-Patraiki v Commission* (Case 11/82), [1985] ECR 207 the applicants sought to challenge a decision which allowed France to impose a tax on yarn imported from Greece. The court held that the applicants who had entered into contracts before the date of the decision were individually concerned and consequently had *locus standi*. The other applicants who had not entered into contracts before the date of the decision were not granted *locus standi*. The applicants who were granted locus standi formed a closed class of individuals as they were fixed and ascertainable at the time the decision was passed.

Recent Case Law on 'Individual Concern'

[9.09] The court has refused to relax the requirements for 'individual concern' and this has resulted in large numbers of non-privileged applicants being denied the opportunity to challenge EU acts.

In *Greenpeace* (Case 321/95 P), [1998] ECR I–1651 the court re-affirmed the *Plaumann* test and held that the applicants had not shown that they were 'individually concerned'.

Following the *Greenpeace* decision two attempts were made to relax the 'individual concern' requirements.

In *Unión des Pequeños Agricultores* (Case 50/00 P), [2002] ECR I–6677 Advocate-General Jacobs stated at para 98 of his opinion that the restrictive interpretation of direct and individual concern seemed 'increasingly untenable in light of the Court's case law on the principle of effective judicial protection'. At para 60, he recommended a new test for individual concern whereby an applicant would have 'individual concern' when 'the measure has, or is liable to have, a substantial adverse effect on his interests'.

However the court did not follow Advocate-General Jacobs' opinion.

In *Jégo-Quéré* (Case T–177/01), [2002] ECR II–2365 the Court of First Instance (now the General Court) put forward a new test for 'individual concern'. The court stated at para 51 that:

> 'A natural or legal person is to be regarded as individually concerned by a Community measure of general application that concerns him directly if the measure in question affects his legal position, in a manner which is both definite and immediate, by restricting his rights or by imposing obligations on him. The number and position of other persons who are likewise affected by the measure, or who may be so, are of no relevance in that regard.'

The test outlined in *Jégo-Quéré* is more restrictive than the test proposed by Advocate-General Jacobs, however it highlights once again that the current test for individual concern needs to updated. The possibility of change was short-lived however, as the Commission lodged an appeal against the decision in *Jégo-Quéré*. The Court of Justice upheld the Commission's appeal and the test established for individual concern in *Plaumann* was re-affirmed.

Chapter 10

EU Environmental Law

INTRODUCTION

[10.01] The Treaty of Rome did not include any provisions on environmental law and in the absence of any clear policies environmental protection within the Member States was disparate. It was acknowledged that the creation of an internal market would impact the environment but there was confusion as to how it would be possible to harmonise the internal market rules and environmental legislation. The EU has attempted to create harmony through Treaty provisions, however it is still difficult to achieve a balance between protecting the environment and encouraging market growth.

Environmental law was first mentioned in 1967 in the First Common Market Directive (64/548/EEC). This Directive dealt with the various standards for classifying packaging and labelling dangerous goods. In 1972, a decision was made at the UN Stockholm Environment Conference to prepare an environmental policy. Following on from this the EEC's first Environmental Action Programme was published in 1973. Between 1973 and 1986 the EU issued a number of directives in the areas of air, waste pollution and water, and the first reference to the environment in a Treaty was in 1987 through the Single European Act. The incorporation of environmental provisions into the Treaty allowed for growth and development within the area of environmental legislation.

In 1992, the Maastricht Treaty introduced procedural changes for environmental legislation and it also listed sustainable growth as one of the EU's objectives. The Amsterdam Treaty in 1997 brought more changes and the objective of sustainable growth was replaced by the provision for sustainable development. The Lisbon Treaty affirms and clarifies the concept of sustainable development. Article 3 of the Lisbon Treaty states:

> 'the Union ... shall work for the sustainable development of Europe based on balanced economic growth and price stability, a highly competitive social market economy, aiming at full employment and social progress, and a high level of protection and improvement of the quality of the environment'.

EU Environmental Policy is driven by the European Environmental Agency and the European institutions all contribute to the development and implementation of the policy. The European Parliament in particular plays a significant role in highlighting environmental issues.

The EU is constantly aiming to develop environmental awareness. In 2010 the European Commission established a new Director General for Climate Action and the EU has developed future environmental policy through a series of action programmes. The most recent programme is the Seventh Environment Action Programme (EAP) which will be advancing EU environmental policy until 2020. In this programme the Commission identifies three main objectives:

- to protect, conserve and enhance the Union's natural capital;
- to turn the Union into a resource-efficient, green, and competitive low-carbon economy;
- to safeguard the Union's citizens from environment-related pressures and risks to health and wellbeing.

SOURCES OF EU ENVIRONMENTAL LAW

[10.02] European Union environmental law can be found in the following pieces of legislation:

1. the Treaties;
2. secondary legislation;
3. international treaties; and

4.   judgments given by the Court of Justice of the European Union.

Difficulties can often arise in relation to directives. This is due to the fact that directives are drafted in vague language and it can be difficult to judge whether or not a Member State has complied with the requirements of the directive. In addition, directives give a discretion to Member States in the choice and methods of implementation. Despite these difficulties the directive has many benefits for environmental protection and the majority of EU environmental law protection is achieved through directives.

TREATY PROVISIONS

[10.03] Article 191(2) TFEU states that:

> 'Union policy on the environment shall aim at a high level of protection taking into account the diversity of situations in the various regions of the Union. It shall be based on the precautionary principle and on the principles that preventative action should be taken, that environmental damage should as a priority be rectified at source and that the polluter should pay'.

The Court of Justice has applied and developed these principles by examining the wording of the treaty provisions.

THE PRECAUTIONARY PRINCIPLE

[10.04] The precautionary principle seeks to achieve environmental protection through the avoidance of risk.

The General Court of the European Union (formerly the Court of First Instance) has provided some helpful guidance on the application of the precautionary principle.

In *Pfizer Animal Health SA/NV v Council* (Case T–13/99), [2002] ECR II–3305, the precautionary principle was used in order to justify that it was necessary to ban an antibiotic that Pfizer had manufactured due to the fact that there was a possibility of harm for humans. In *UK v Commission* (Case C–180/96), the Commission halted the sale of UK beef due to the potential risk of spreading BSE. The UK opposed the decision taken by the Commission, however they were unsuccessful in their challenge. The Court of Justice stated that EU laws had to be interpreted in line with the precautionary principles and as a result, the Commission's decision to halt the sale of UK beef due to the potential harm for humans was justified.

PREVENTATIVE PRINCIPLE

[10.05] The preventative principle almost always operates in conjunction with the precautionary principle. It is based on preventative decision-making, for example, remove the harm before it causes harm. The preventative principle is extremely important in terms of environmental protection due to the fact that it requires action to be taken at a very early stage before damage occurs.

PROXIMITY PRINCIPLE

[10.06] The proximity principle states that any environmental damage should be rectified at source. The Court of Justice considered the proximity principle in *Commission v Belgium* (Case C–2/90), [1992] ECR I–04431. In this case the court stated that a ban on the import of waste into a particular region could be justified with reference to the proximity principle.

POLLUTER PAYS PRINCIPLE

[10.07] The polluter pays principle requires that any polluter must pay for the damage and cleanup caused by pollution. The polluter pays principle is a strong economic principle that has many benefits for environmental protection. It is believed that the risk of economic loss greatly influences the behaviour of possible polluters.

ENFORCEMENT OF ENVIRONMENTAL LAW

[10.08] The Commission ensures that Treaty obligations are fulfilled pursuant to Art 258 TFEU it can enforce Member States to comply with their EU law obligations. This power also applies to environmental law and consequently the Commission can require Member States to meet their EU environmental law obligations pursuant to Art 258 TFEU. The Commission is often notified of environmental infringements by concerned third parties or individuals.

THE AARHUS CONVENTION

[10.09] The United Nations Economic Commission for Europe (UNECE) drafted the Aarhaus Convention. The Aarhus Convention was adopted on 25 June 1998 and it contains guidelines that promote public participation in the area of environmental protection. The Aarhus Convention has three pillars:

1.   access to environmental information;

2.   participation in environmental decision making;

3.   access to justice in environmental matters.

Access to information allows individuals to access environmental information without having to show an interest in the information that they wish to access. However, requests for access to information must meet the required time limits and a request for access to information can always be refused on the grounds of public interest.

Public participation in decision making applies to planning permission and environmental licensing, eg waste licences. Public authorities engaged in environmental decision-making must publish notices that contain information on the specific licence applications. The notice must also tell the public how they can participate in the decision-making process. If a decision has been made that may affect the environment, members of the public can seek a review of that decision.

Ireland ratified the Aarhus Convention on 20 June 2012. Ireland also ratified the Protocol on pollutant release and transfer registers, and the GMO amendment to the Aarhus Convention. These three agreements entered into force in Ireland on 18 September 2012. In order to implement the Aarhus Convention the European Union issued two directives. The directives are:

1.   Directive 2003/4/EC on public access to environmental information.

2.   Directive 2003/35/EC on public participation.

Ireland has implemented the two directives issued by the European Union and the Aarhus Convention has also been implemented through national legislation.

ENVIRONMENTAL IMPACT ASSESSMENT

[10.10] An environmental impact assessment (EIA) is necessary for certain types of development. The purpose of an environmental impact assessment is to ensure that the impact on the environment is considered before a decision is taken to go ahead with new developments. Directive 85/337/EEC sets out the provisions concerning environmental impact assessments. The initial directive has been amended three times in 1997, 2003 and 2009. In 2011, the three amendments were codified by Directive 2011/92/EU and in 2014 amendments were put in place by Directive 2014/52/EU.

The environmental impact assessment procedure begins with the scoping stage where the developer requests information from the competent authority as to what should be covered in the EIA. The developer then provides the necessary information on the EIA to the competent authority. The information must be made available to the public and this includes public bodies and affected Member States. The competent authority then reaches a decision. The public are informed of the decision and the decision can be challenged in the courts.

The Commission has highlighted Ireland's failure to transpose the Environmental Impact Assessment Directive into national law. The Commission was of the view that Ireland's legislation on environmental impact assessments was not adequate and as a result the Commission referred Ireland to the European Court of Justice. The Commission sought to have a lump sum fine of €1.8m imposed and a daily penalty payment of over €19,000 until Ireland put an end to the infringement. Ireland failed to transpose the directive into national law even though the Court of Justice gave a ruling on the matter in March 2011. Ireland gave an undertaking to adopt the necessary legislation by May 2012, however the legislation was not adopted and as a result the Commission referred the matter back to the Court of Justice. On 19 December 2012, the Court of Justice ordered Ireland to pay a lump sum of €1.5m for failing to comply with its obligations to transpose the EIA Directive. The court took into account the fact that Ireland's ability to pay was diminished due to the economic crisis when assessing the lump sum figure.

EU ENVIRONMENTAL LITIGATION – ACTIONS AGAINST MEMBER STATES

[10.11] The Commission receives most of its information about environmental infringements from individuals. The Commission has an environmental complaints system in place and this allows individuals to place a complaint when they feel there has been an infringement of EU environmental laws. An individual cannot force the Commission to take an action against a Member State. The Commission has a discretion when it decides to take action under Art 258 TFEU. An individual can only have a complaint addressed through the Commission and an individual has to accept the Commission's decision to act or not to act.

If the Commission takes an action against a Member State for failure to meet EU environmental law obligations the Court of Justice does not inform the Member State how to meet its environmental obligations. The result will be that the Member State has to comply with the Commission's decision. A Member State can be subject to penalties pursuant to Art 260 TFEU. In *Commission v Greece* (Case C–387/97), [2000] ECR I–5047, Greece failed to implement a management plan for toxic waste in Crete. As a result of this breach, Greece had to pay a £20,000 fine daily until the EU law obligations were met. In *Commission v Spain* (Case 278/01), [2003] ECR I–14141, Spain was forced to pay an annual penalty for breaching the bathing water directive.

IRISH INFRINGEMENTS

[10.12] In *Commission v Ireland* (Case C–494/01), [2005] ECR I–3331, Ireland's obligations under the waste framework directive came under scrutiny. Between 1997 and 2000 the Commission received 12 different complaints concerning waste management in Ireland. In 2001, the Commission issued a reasoned opinion outlining the details of the 12 complaints and alleged that Ireland had failed generally to fulfil the obligations arising under the waste framework directive. The Commission was not satisfied with Ireland's response to the reasoned opinion and it brought an action against Ireland for failure to fulfil obligations before the Court of Justice.

The court found that Ireland had allowed illegal dumping by not ensuring that all municipal landfills held the necessary permit required by the directive. In addition, the Irish authorities had allowed unauthorised activities in numerous places over long periods of time and the Irish authorities failed to insist that those activities were brought to an end. The court also pointed out that Ireland was late in transposing the directive and the procedure for obtaining a permit was extremely slow. It could take anywhere between 808 days to 4 years to obtain a permit.

The court found that Ireland had failed to fulfil its obligations in a general and persistent nature, and as a result it had failed to fulfil its obligations under the waste framework directive.

In *Commission v Ireland* (Case C–374/11) the court was of the view that Ireland had not correctly transposed the Directive on the disposal of waste waters (Council Directive 75/442/EEC as amended by Council Directive 91/156/EEC). As a result, the court imposed a penalty payment of €12,000 for each day of non-compliance and a lump sum fine of €2m.

[10.13] The implementation and enforcement of EU environmental law in Ireland continues to cause problems. Ireland is not the only Member State with these difficulties and the Environment Directorate-General has the highest number of open cases in the Commission. Environmental directives contribute to this problem due to their vague and general terms, and as a result it is often impossible to adequately identify Member States' obligations. It is a fundamental principle of EU law that directives give Member States a discretion for implementation. However, due to this fact problems will continue to arise with the implementation and enforcement of environmental directives.

ACTIONS AGAINST THE COMMISSION AND COUNCIL

[10.14] Actions against the Commission and the Council for failure to meet environmental law obligations can be brought pursuant to the Aarhus Convention and also pursuant to Art 263 TFEU. The *locus standi* requirements can greatly hinder actions in this regard as can be seen from the following case law.

In *Stitchting Greenpeace Council v Commission* (Case C –321/95 P), [1998] ECR 1651, the Commission had granted funding to Spain for the construction of two power stations. Greenpeace and a group of interested parties sought to challenge this decision and stated that it was a breach of EU environmental law. Greenpeace and the group of interested parties were unable to establish *locus standi* due to the fact that the court said the decision did not individually concern them. The substantive matter of the environmental infringements were never addressed because Greenpeace and the interested parties were unable to establish standing. This case highlights the difficulties in bringing successful environmental law infringement challenges against the Council or the Commission. It seems that it will be impossible to establish standing in the future if bodies such as Greenpeace are unable to establish individual concern.

The court has refused to relax its strict interpretation and this was demonstrated in the case of *Markku Sahlstedt and Others v Commission* (Case C–362/06 P), [2009] ECR I–2903. This case concerned Council Directive 92/43/EC on the conservation of natural habitats and of wild flora and fauna – the Habitats Directive. Pursuant to the Habitats Directive each Member State must draw up and publish a list of important ecological sites. In addition, it is the responsibility of each Member State to ensure that the environment is protected in the outlined areas. The areas would then be known as Special Areas of Conservation (SAC). A group of farmers from Finland brought an action seeking to annul the decision that allowed for the creation of SACs. The group failed to meet the *locus standi* requirements and the court held that the applicants were not directly concerned by the decision. The applicants appealed this decision to the Court of Justice. Advocate General Bosch stated that the land owners and farmers had established individual concern, however the Court of Justice did not follow the Advocate General's opinion. The Court affirmed the previous decision and stated that the applicants were not individually concerned.

Chapter 11

Free Movement of Goods

INTRODUCTION

[11.01] The European Union was established primarily with a view to generating trade between the Member States. In order to increase trade between the Member States it was necessary to remove any restrictions or barriers that existed. Custom duties and similar charges that existed in Member States were prohibited to allow the free movement of goods within the European Union. As a result all traders were able to compete equally based on the price and quality of their goods without being subject to national restrictions.

The free movement of goods provisions are found in Arts 28–37 TFEU. The provisions prohibit the following:

- custom duties on imports and exports;

- charges that have the equivalent effect as custom duties;

- quantitative restrictions on imports and exports; and

- measures that have the equivalent effect as quantitative restrictions.

THE DEFINITION OF GOODS

[11.02] There is no definition in the treaties for the term 'goods' or 'products'. The Court of Justice provided the following definition in *Commission v Italy* (Case C–7/68), [1968] ECR 423.

> 'By goods, within the meaning of [Art 28 TFEU], there must be understood products which can be valued in money and which are capable, as such, of forming the subject of commercial transactions'.

CUSTOM DUTIES

[11.03] Article 30 TFEU prohibits all custom duties and charges that have the equivalent effect as a custom duty. A custom duty or equivalent charge is a revenue payment on imported goods. These types of charges are prohibited because imported goods are then more expensive than similar goods that are not imported. The prohibition outlined in Art 30 TFEU is absolute and a Member State cannot derogate from the prohibition.

JUSTIFICATION FOR CUSTOM DUTIES

[11.04] If a Member State imposes a custom duty or a charge that has the equivalent effect they are in breach of Art 30 TFEU. There is no defence in the treaties for a breach of Art 30 TFEU. However, the Court of Justice has outlined three situations when a charge may be lawful:

1. Charges for services rendered;

2. Charges for inspections that are imposed by EU Law;

3. Charges that relate to Art 110 TFEU and the internal tax system.

QUANTITATIVE RESTRICTIONS

[11.05] Article 34 and 35 TFEU prohibit quantitative restrictions on imports and exports and measures that have the equivalent effect. The Treaty provisions are as follows;

Article 34 (ex Article 28 TEC)

Quantitative restrictions on imports and all measures having equivalent effect shall be prohibited between Member States.

Article 35 (ex Article 29 TEC)

Quantitative restrictions on exports, and all measures having equivalent effect, shall be prohibited between Member States.

Case law on Quantitative Restrictions

[11.06] The main body of case law concerns Art 34 TFEU that prohibits restrictions on imports.

Quantitative restrictions were defined by the Court of Justice in *Riseria Luigi Geddo v Ente Nazionale Risi* (Case 2/73), [1973] ECR 865 as 'measures which amount to a total or partial restraint of imports exports or goods in transit'.

Measures that have an equivalent effect as quantitative restrictions (MEQRs) are not as easy to identify. The Court of Justice provided a definition for MEQRs in *Procureur du Roi v Dassonville* (Case 8/74), [1974] ECR 837. The *Dassonville* case concerned a Belgian law that required all imported goods to carry a certificate of origin from the state where the goods were manufactured. Dassonville imported Scotch whiskey from France with a view to selling it in Belgium. The whiskey was sold in Belgium without an official certificate of origin from the UK. It was argued that the Belgian law requirement was contrary to EU law. The Court of Justice held that the Belgian law was a MEQR and provided the following definition for MEQRs:

> 'All trading rules enacted by Member States which are capable of hindering, directly or indirectly, actually or potentially, intra-Community trade are to be considered as measures having an effect equivalent to quantitative restrictions'

The *Dassonville* definition was broad and all encompassing. The Court of Justice refined the definition in *Rewe-Zentral AG v Bundesmonopolverwaltung fur Branntwein* (Case 120/78), [1979] ECR 649 (the *Cassis de Dijon* case). This case concerned a German law that required a minimum alcohol content of 25 per cent for certain liqueurs. The French liqueur Cassis de Dijon only had an alcohol content of between 15–20 per cent. As a result of the German requirement Cassis de Dijon could not be imported into Germany. It was argued that the requirement under German law was an MEQR even though it applied to both imported and domestic goods.

The Court of Justice made a distinction between distinctly and indistinctly applicable measures:

- Distinctly applicable measures only apply to imported goods;
- Indistinctly applicable measures apply to both imported and domestic goods.

[11.07] The following two principles were established by the court.

1. The Rule of Reason

Restrictions that meet certain mandatory requirements <u>are allowed</u> for indistinctly applicable measures. The court listed mandatory requirements as:

- effectiveness of fiscal supervision;
- protection of Public Health;
- fairness of commercial transactions; and
- defence of the consumer.

This list is not exhaustive and only provides examples of mandatory requirements.

2. Principle of Mutual Recognition

Goods cannot be prevented from being introduced to a Member State if the goods were lawfully produced and marketed in another Member State. However the principle of mutual recognition will be set aside if the rule of reason applies.

The two principles established by the Court of Justice in the *Cassis de Dijon* case highlight the fact that the *Dassonville* definition was too broad. The Court's decision shows that it is sometimes necessary to excuse indistinctly applicable measures from the all-encompassing nature of the *Dassonville* definition.

Indistinctly applicable measures were considered further in *Keck and Mithouard* (Case C–267/91), [1993] ECR I–6097. This case concerned a French law that prohibited the resale of goods at a loss. It was argued that the French law violated the free movement of goods provisions. The Court of Justice took the opportunity to modify the principle on indistinctly applicable measures. The court held that if a measure was indistinctly applicable and if the measure was a 'selling arrangement' then the measure would not breach Art 28 TEC (now Art 34 TFEU). The 'selling arrangement' is only lawful if both domestic and imported products are affected in the same way, as this means there is no discrimination against imported products.

The *Keck and Mithouard* judgment only applies to 'selling arrangements' involving the advertising and marketing of goods. The judgment does not apply to restrictions on the actual goods such as labelling or packaging restrictions. Furthermore, if the restriction only discriminates imported products it is an MEQR.

ARTICLE 36 TFEU EXCEPTIONS

[11.08] Article 36 TFEU allows the free movement of goods to be legitimately restricted by Member States. Article 36 states the following:

> 'The provisions of Articles 34 and 35 shall not preclude prohibitions or restrictions on imports, exports or goods in transit justified on grounds of public morality, public policy or public security; the protection of health and life of humans, animals or plants; the protection of national treasures possessing artistic, historic or archaeological value; or the protection of industrial and commercial property. Such prohibitions or restrictions shall not, however, constitute a means of arbitrary discrimination or a disguised restriction on trade between Member States.'

Member States can derogate from the provisions of Arts 34 and 35 TFEU if their actions come within one of the grounds listed in Art 36 TFEU. The Court of Justice has interpreted the six grounds in Art 36 TFEU very restrictively. The grounds are exhaustive and the list can only be increased by a treaty amendment. Member States cannot use the grounds as a means of arbitrary discrimination or disguised restrictions. A Member State that seeks to rely on Art 36 TFEU has the burden of proving that a restriction comes within one of the grounds listed in Art 36 TFEU.

Public Morality

[11.09] In the case of *R v Henn and Darby* (Case 34/79), [1979] ECR 3795 the defendants imported pornographic material into the UK from the Netherlands. Importing pornographic films and magazines was prohibited under UK customs law. It was argued by the UK that the customs law was justified on the grounds of public morality. The Court of Justice accepted this argument and held that 'it is for each Member State to determine in accordance with its own scale of values and in the form selected by it the requirements of public morality in its territory'.

Although there was a breach of Art 34 TFEU the restriction was justified under Art 36 TFEU.

The area of public morality was also considered in *Conegate v Customs & Excise* (Case 12/85), [1986] ECR 1007. Customs authorities in the UK seized a consignment of life size inflatable dolls that had been imported from Germany. It was argued that the seizure by customs was an infringement of the free movement of goods provisions. The UK argued that the seizure was justified on the grounds of public morality. However the UK had restrictions on the sale of similar goods but there were no restrictions on the manufacture of such goods. The Court of Justice held that the UK could not rely on the public morality ground. The seizure constituted an arbitrary discrimination as UK companies could manufacture and market similar goods lawfully.

Public Policy

[11.10] This principle was considered in *Cullet v Leclerc* (Case 231/83), [1985] ECR 305 by Advocate General Verloren Van Themartt. He stated that the acceptance of civil disturbance as a justification for encroachments upon the free movement of goods would have unacceptable drastic consequences. The consequences would be that private interest groups could determine the scope of the freedoms provided for in the treaties.

The public policy exception has wide potential and as a result it has been construed strictly by the court.

Public Security

[11.11] This ground was successfully relied upon in *Campus Oil Ltd v Minister for Industry and Energy* (Case 72/83), [1984] ECR 2727. This case concerned Irish legislation that required all petrol importers to purchase a proportion of their petrol requirements from the state-owned refinery at a price fixed by the Minister. The Court of Justice held that this requirement was justified on public security grounds. The state oil refinery would be in danger of going out of business without this compulsory purchase rule. The Irish legislation ensured the continued existence of the oil refinery and this would guarantee a supply of oil to the Irish State at all times.

The Protection of the Health and Life of Humans, Animals and Plants

[11.12] This ground was considered in the case of *Officier van Justitie v Sandoz BV* (Case 174/82), [1983] ECR 2445. The Dutch authorities placed a ban on certain foods that contained added vitamins due to a belief that the vitamins were dangerous. The vitamins themselves were not dangerous however over consumption of food containing the vitamins could be dangerous. The Court of Justice held that it was for Member States to decide on the appropriate level of public health protection.

However, in *Commission v Germany* (Case 178/84), [1987] ECR 1227 the German authorities placed a ban on additives in beer and this was found to be contrary to the free movement of goods.

Protection of National Treasures Possessing Artistic, Historic or Archaeological Value

[11.13] This exception was referred to in *Commission v Italy* (Case C–7/68), [1968] ECR 423. The court stated that a quantitative restriction on the export of art treasures was justified but that a tax charge could not be justified. This case was ultimately decided under Art 30 TFEU.

Protection of Industrial and Commercial Property

[11.14] Industrial and commercial property relates to patents, trademarks, copyright and design rights. In *Deutsche Grammophon Gesellschaft v Metro-SB-Grossmarkte GmbH* (Case C–78/70), [1971] ECR 487 the court stated the following;

> 'If a right related to copyright is relied upon to prevent the marketing in a Member State of products distributed by the holder of the right or with his consent on the territory of another Member State on the sole ground that such distribution did not take place on the national territory, such a prohibition, which would legitimize the isolation of national markets, would be repugnant to the essential purpose of the Treaty, which is to unite national markets into a single market.'

That purpose could not be attained if, under the various legal systems of the Member States, nationals of those states were able to partition the market and bring about arbitrary discrimination or disguised restrictions on trade between Member States.

Chapter 12

The Free Movement of Persons

INTRODUCTION

[12.01] The free movement of persons provisions were developed to promote economic activity within the European Union. The provisions complemented and enhanced the European Union's economic focus. The original treaty provisions on free movement granted workers the right to travel and take up employment within the European Union without discrimination on the grounds of nationality. Workers also enjoyed the same rights and benefits as nationals of the Member States.

The free movement provisions have been extended to include family members, students, retired persons and persons of independent means. The free movement provisions are now all found in the Treaty on the Functioning of the European Union. The provisions on the free movement of workers are contained in Art 45 TFEU. The rights of the self-employed are contained in Art 49 TFEU and the rights of persons providing services are contained in Art 56 TFEU.

Citizenship of the European Union was introduced by the Treaty on European Union (TEU) and free movement rights were granted to all citizens of the European Union. The provisions on Union citizenship are contained in Arts 20 and 21 TFEU.

The Treaty provisions are supplemented by secondary legislation and a consolidation of all the free movement directives is contained in the Citizenship Directive 2004/38. The Treaty provisions on free movement and citizenship operate in conjunction with the Citizenship Directive 2004/38.

The free movement and citizenship provisions are not absolute and they are subject to conditions and limitations. Member States can restrict free movement on the grounds of public policy, public security and public health.

FREE MOVEMENT OF WORKERS

[12.02] Article 45 TFEU contains the provisions on the free movement of workers

> '1. Freedom of movement for workers shall be secured within the Union.
>
> 2. Such freedom of movement shall entail the abolition of any discrimination based on nationality between workers of the Member States as regards employment, remuneration and other conditions of work and employment.
>
> 3. It shall entail the right, subject to limitations justified on grounds of public policy, public security or public health:
>
> (a)   to accept offers of employment actually made;
>
> (b)   to move freely within the territory of Member States for this purpose;
>
> (c)   to stay in a Member State for the purpose of employment in accordance with the provisions governing the employment of nationals of that State laid down by law, regulation or administrative action;
>
> (d)   to remain in the territory of a Member State after having been employed in that State, subject to conditions which shall be embodied in regulations to be drawn up by the Commission.
>
> 4. The provisions of this Article shall not apply to employment in the public service.'

Article 45 TFEU contains the provisions that entitle workers to move freely within the European Union without any risk of discrimination based on nationality. The provision focuses predominantly on a worker within the European Union, however the term worker is not defined. It is very important to establish who is a worker for the purpose of Art 45 TFEU. If an individual is a worker they will be protected by the broad range of rights contained in the provisions.

Definition of 'Worker'

[12.03] There is no Treaty definition for the term 'worker' and the Court of Justice has developed the definition through its case law. The court has stated that the term worker must not be defined by national standards and that instead a European meaning would be applied to the definition. The term worker has been afforded a broad interpretation by the Court of Justice.

In *Levin v Staatsecretaris van Justi* (Case C–53/81), [1982] ECR 1035 the court looked at the position of a British national who was living in the Netherlands and working part time. Leven was refused a residency permit because her wages were less than the minimum required wage. The Court of Justice held that a part-time worker will be entitled to move and reside as a worker once the work in which they are engaged in is an effective and genuine economic activity.

In *Lawrie Blum v Land BadenWurttemberg* (Case C–66/85), [1986] ECR 2121 the court held that a trainee teacher was a worker for the purpose of the provisions as she was performing a service of economic value and was receiving a measure of remuneration for that work.

In *Kempf v Staatsecretaris van Justi* (Case C 139/85), [1986] ECR 1741 the applicant was a German national living in the Netherlands. He was working for 12 hours per week giving music lessons and his income was supplemented by state welfare. When Kempf applied for a residency permit his application was refused. The government was of the opinion that he was not engaged in proper work as he was claiming social assistance. The Court of Justice did not agree with this decision and held that hours worked and income were only contributing factors when assessing if the work was genuine and effective.

[12.04] The question then arises as to how unpaid work should be classified.

In *Steymann v Staatsecretaris van Justi* (Case 196/87), [1988] ECR 6159 a German national joined a religious community in the

Netherlands and worked for the community as a plumber. In addition to doing plumbing work, Steymann also helped with general housework. He did not receive any formal wages for his activities, his work went towards his upkeep. The Court of Justice held that even though Steymann did not receive any formal wages for his work, his work was still an effective and genuine economic activity.

A limitation was placed on the term 'worker' in *Bettray v Staatsecretaris van Justi* (Case C–344/87), [1989] ECR 1621 Bettray was participating in a drug rehabilitation scheme and his work was both paid and supervised. The Court of Justice held that a person participating in a drug rehabilitation scheme was not a worker due to the fact that the work focused on reintegration into the workplace and as such it could not be regarded as a genuine and effective economic activity.

Family Members and Dependants of Workers

[12.05] The free movement provisions are supplemented by secondary legislation that entitles family members of the worker to move and reside with the worker. The provisions covering a worker's family are now contained in Directive 2004/38. The rights of a worker's family are wholly dependent on the rights of the worker.

In the case *Netherlands v Reed* (Case C–59/85), [1986] ECR 1283, Reed had travelled to the Netherlands from Britain in an attempt to find work. She was unable to find employment but moved in with Mr W who was British and working in the Netherlands. When Reid applied for a residence permit she was refused on the grounds that under Dutch law a non-national could only extend their right of residence to a co-habitee if the relationship was in existence before they moved to the Netherlands. The court held that the term 'spouse' included co-habitee and since Dutch nationals were entitled to live with a non-national co-habitee, irrespective of whether their relationship had begun in the Netherlands or not, a non-national must receive the same treatment as a Dutch national.

FREE MOVEMENT OF THE SELF-EMPLOYED

[12.06] Article 49 TFEU provides for the right of establishment and Art 56 TFEU sets out the provisions for the freedom to provide services. These two rights apply to individuals and companies. The freedom of establishment allows an individual to set up a business as a self-employed person in one of the 28 Member States. A person can be established in one Member State and then travel to another Member State in order to provide a service. When a person does this it constitutes the provision of a service.

Article 49 TFEU states that restrictions on the freedom of establishment of nationals of a Member State in the territory of another Member State shall be prohibited. Freedom of establishment includes the right to take up and pursue activities as self-employed persons and to set up and manage undertakings.

Article 56 TFEU states that restrictions on the freedom to provide services within the Union shall be prohibited in respect of nationals of Member States who are established in a Member State other than that of the person for whom the services are intended.

THE RIGHT OF ESTABLISHMENT

[12.07] Article 49 TFEU works in conjunction with Art 18 TFEU the provision that prohibits discrimination on the grounds of nationality. The purpose of Art 49 TFEU is to ensure that the self-employed are treated equally with the nationals of a host Member State. The underlying principle is non-discrimination. However, it can be difficult to treat professional conduct and qualifications equally. This often happens when an individual meets their home state requirements but then they find a host state's requirements are different and impossible to meet.

The difficulty in relation to professional conduct was considered in *Gebhard v Consiglio del Ordine degli Avocati e Procuratori di Milano* (Case C–55/94), [1995] ECR 1–4165. Mr Gebhard was a German national who qualified as a lawyer in Germany. He moved to Milan and established his own legal practice. The Bar Council prohibited Mr Gebhard from practicing law in Italy whilst using the title Avocato. The Court of Justice stated that national rules imposing restrictions on the freedom of establishment are justified in order to ensure that legal activities are carried out correctly. The court went on to state that if a national measure was liable to hinder or make less attractive the exercise of the freedom of establishment the measure must fulfil four conditions. According to the judgment the four conditions are that the measure must:

1. be applied in a non-discriminatory manner;

2. must be justified by imperative requirements in the general interest;

3. they must be suitable for securing the attainment of their objectives;

4. they must not go beyond what is necessary in order to attain the goals.

RULES IN RELATION TO PROFESSIONAL QUALIFICATIONS

[12.08] The professional qualification requirements can vary from member state to member state. As a result professionals can often find themselves in a situation where their free movement is restricted due to the national states rules on professional qualifications. In *Thieffry v Consile de l'Ordre des Avocats a la Cour de Paris*, (Case C–71/76), [1977] ECR 765, Thieffry was a Belgian national who completed a law degree at a Belgian university. Thieffry then sought admission to the Paris Bar, however his admission was refused due to the fact that he did not hold a French law degree. The Court ruled that this was indirect discrimination pursuant to Art 49 TFEU and it was an unjustified restriction on the freedom of establishment.

FREEDOM TO PROVIDE SERVICES

[12.09] Article 57 TFEU states that services shall be considered to be services within the meaning of the Treaties where they are normally provided for remuneration insofar as they are not governed by the provisions relating to freedom of movement of goods, capital and persons. Services shall, in particular, include:

(a) activities of an industrial character;

(b) activities of a commercial character;

(c) activities of craftsmen; and

(d) activities of the professions.

Restrictions on the Freedom to Provide Services

[12.10] Difficulties can arise when the provision of a service directly contravenes a host state's rules on certain activities. If this occurs a Member State may impose restrictions on the freedom to provide services. This issue was considered in *Society for the Protection of Unborn Children Ltd (SPUC) v Grogan* (Case C–159/90), [1991] ECR 1–4685. In Ireland it is illegal to provide abortion services and this case concerned a group of students in Ireland who were providing information on abortion services that were available in England. The question arose as to whether the student's activities were a provision of a service within the definition of Art 57 TFEU. The court held that abortion services did come within the provisions of Art 57 TFEU, however as the student's activity was not remunerated the requisite economic link had not been established.

In *Sager v Dennemeyer & Co Ltd* (Case C–76/90), [1991] ECR I–4221 the court stated that the provision of services may be limited by rules which are justified on the grounds of public interest. The court went on to say that the restrictions must be objectively necessary in order to ensure compliance with the professional rules and must not exceed what is necessary to attain these objectives.

DIRECTIVE 2006/123/EC ON SERVICES

[12.11] The Services Directive seeks to remedy the difficulties that arise due to the various Member States rules on professional conduct and professional qualifications. The objectives of the Directive are broad and they seek to remove barriers on the freedom of establishment and the provision of services, however the Directive does exclude a wide number of services and it does contain a number of derogations.

The rights of family members are contained in Directive 2004/38. Family members of a worker have the right to move and install themselves with the worker. The right of residence for family members is not an independent right and it is derived from the right of residence of the worker. However Art 13(2)(a) of Directive 2004/38 provides that annulment of a marriage or partnership will not result in the automatic loss of the right of residence. This provision comes with a proviso that the partnership lasted for at least three years prior to annulment.

In *Diatta v Land Berlin* (Case C–267/83), [1985] ECR 567, the wife of a worker was found to still have a right of residence even though she had separated and had started living separately from her husband.

CITIZENSHIP OF THE EUROPEAN UNION

[12.12] Citizenship of the European Union was created by the Treaty on European Union (TEU). The Court of Justice used this new found status as the basis for developing the free movement provisions.

In *Sala v Freistat Bayern* (Case C–85/96), [1998] ECR 1/2691 the Court established that citizens are entitled to rely on the free movement provisions irrespective of whether or not they are workers. Sala was a Spanish national who had been living in Germany since 1968. She had been employed at different times throughout her time in Germany but had been receiving social assistance since 1989. She had been obtaining residence permits regularly from the German government. However from 1984 onwards she only had documents which stated that her residency permit had been applied for. Once again in 1994 Sala received her residency permit. The issue under consideration in the case was that in 1993 Sala applied for a child raising allowance and at this point she did not have her residency permit. Her application for a child raising allowance was refused on the basis that she was not a German national and she did not have a residency entitlement or permit. Sala claimed that such a refusal contravened EU law. The Court of Justice held that where a non-national is discriminated against when nationals in the same situation were not, it is discrimination. The court also stated that Sala could rely on the Treaty provisions due the fact that she was a citizen of the European Union.

The case of *Rudy Grzelczyk v Centre Public d'Aide Sociale d'ottignes-Louvain-la–Neuve (CPAS)* (Case C–184/99), [2001] ECR I–6193, concerned a French national who was studying in Belgium. During his first three years of study he worked part-time. When he reached fourth year he decided not to work and applied to the CPAS for a Minimex payment, which is a non-contributory minimum subsistence allowance. Initially the CPAS granted him this allowance however the Belgian minister made a decision that, as Grzelczyk was not a Belgian national he was not entitled to the allowance. As a result of this the CPAS stopped all payments to Grzelczyk. The court did not treat the case as if Grzelczyk was a worker but they saw it as an issue of citizenship. The court went on to say that 'Union citizenship is destined to be the fundamental status of nationals of the Member States'.

In *Baumbast v Secretary of State for the Home Department* (Case C–413–99), [2002] ECR I–7091, Baumbast was a German national who had been working and living in the UK. Baumbast was refused a residency permit on the grounds that he was no longer working in the United Kingdom. The Court of Justice stated that Union citizenship gave rise to residency rights. In this case Baumbast would not become a burden on the state and as a result it would be disproportionate to not give him residency rights.

In *Orr v London Borough of Ealing and Secretary of State for Education Ex Parte Bidar*, (Case C–209/03), [2005] ECR I–2119, Bidar was a French national who had travelled to the UK with his mother. Bidar's mother died shortly after they arrived in the UK and he then completed his secondary education in the UK whilst living with his grandmother. Bidar started a university course in London and applied for a student loan. However, his student loan was rejected due to the fact that he was not settled in the UK. The Court of Justice said that as a result of Union citizenship, Bidar was entitled to equal treatment with nationals regarding the student loan.

[12.13] The case of *Zhu and Chen v Secretary of State for the Home Department* (Case C–200/2), [2004] ECR I–9925 demonstrates the significance of the citizenship provisions and how the court is prepared to develop them in order to enhance the free movement provisions. In this case Mrs Chen and her husband were both Chinese nationals. Mr Chen was the director and majority shareholder of a Chinese company. In the course of his work, Mr Chen spent a lot of time in Europe and particularly in the United Kingdom. The couple's first child was a Chinese national and in May 2000 Mrs Chen travelled to the United Kingdom to give birth to their second child. Following legal advice she travelled to Belfast in July 2000 and her second child, Catherine, was born there on 16 September 2000.

Before the amendment to the Irish Constitution in 2004 any person born in Ireland was entitled to Irish nationality under s 6(1) of the Irish Nationality and Citizenship Act 1956, which was amended in 2001 and applies retroactively from 2 December 1999.

As a result of this law in September 2000 Catherine was issued with an Irish passport. Catherine was not entitled to British nationality as birth alone in the United Kingdom does not automatically confer nationality. It was not disputed that Mrs Chen deliberately moved to Northern Ireland in order for her second child to acquire Irish nationality and as a result acquire the right to reside in the United Kingdom.

After Mrs Chen and her daughter were refused a long-term residency permit in the UK where they were living, they lodged an appeal. The court was asked by Immigration Appellate Authority whether under Community Law Mrs Chen and her daughter, Catherine, had a right to reside in the United Kingdom.

Firstly, the court looked at Catherine's right of residence and stated that every citizen of the European Union has the right to reside in another Member State under the EC Treaty, subject to limitations and conditions laid down by the Treaty and provisions adopted for its implementation. The court acknowledged that Member States may require nationals of another Member State who wish to live in their state, to have medical insurance for themselves and their family and sufficient resources to ensure they do not become a burden on the social assistance scheme of the host state. In this case Catherine had medical insurance and sufficient resources, which were provided by her mother and as a result would not become a burden on the United Kingdom social assistance scheme.

The court went on to state that it was irrelevant that Catherine did not possess the required resources herself as there was no Community law stating where the origin of such resources should be. In addition the provisions which promote the free movement of persons, which is a fundamental right, have to be broadly interpreted.

The court also considered the fact that Mrs Chen deliberately moved to Northern Ireland in order for her child to be an Irish national. The court clearly expressed that Catherine's application for a residency permit could not be rejected purely because she deliberately acquired Irish nationality in order to obtain a right of residency in the United Kingdom under Community law as a national of a Member State. The court said that nationality was a concern for each Member State and one Member State could not restrict the effects of the nationality granted by another Member State.

The court was of the opinion that Catherine's right of residency would be totally ineffective if Mrs Chen's right to reside with her daughter in the UK was refused. The court held that Mrs Chen was entitled to residence since the only way Catherine could enjoy her right of residency was to be accompanied by her mother who was her carer.

[12.14] In *Akrich* (Case C–109/01), [2003] ECR I–9607, the focus was on the residency rights of a Moroccan national. Akrich, a Moroccan national, had been deported from the United Kingdom. However he returned to the United Kingdom illegally and married a British citizen. Akrich's wife moved to Ireland in 1997 and when Akrich was being deported from the UK again he sought to be deported to Ireland due to the fact that his spouse was residing there. He was deported to Ireland in 1997 and he and his wife resided there until 1998. Akrich's spouse was offered a job in the United Kingdom in 1998 and as a result Akrich and his wife wanted to return to the UK. Akrich sought to revoke the deportation order and he applied to remain in the United Kingdom in his capacity as a British citizen's spouse.

Mr Akrich relied on the judgment of *Singh* (Case C–370/90), [1992] ECR I–4265, the Singh case had established that a national of a member state who had worked in another member state was entitled to return to their own country accompanied by their spouse irrespective of the nationality of that spouse. The UK had established through investigations that Mr and Mrs Akrich were seeking to return to the UK as they were aware of their rights under EU law. As a result, the investigations the application was refused by the UK. The UK stated that the couple had resided in Ireland purely to establish a right of residence for Mr Akrich in the UK.

The matter was referred to the Court of Justice and the court held that the motives underlying a move to another Member State are irrelevant, even if the purpose of the move is to establish a right of residence. The court also stated that a spouse has the right to install himself with a citizen of the Union provided that he is lawfully resident in a Member State when he moves to another Member State. However, the court did say that there would be an abuse if the marriage was one of convenience and was not genuine.

[12.15] The court refined the *Akrich* judgment in *Metock* (Case C–127/08). This case focused on the Irish legislation that transposed Directive 2004/38/EC on the right of citizens of the Union and their family members to move and reside freely within the territory of the Member States. The Irish legislation provides that a national of a third country who is a family member of a Union citizen may reside with or join that citizen on condition that he or she is lawfully resident in another Member State. A third country national is a person who is not a national of one of the 28 Member States of the European Union. It was argued that the Irish legislation was not compatible with the Directive. This case concerned third-country nationals who were seeking asylum in Ireland. While the third-country nationals were residing in Ireland, they met and married citizens of the European Union who were residing in Ireland. The marriages were clearly established as not being marriages of convenience. Following the marriage the third-country nationals applied for residency pursuant to being the spouse of a Union citizen. The Minister for Justice refused the applications for residency on the basis that the essential criteria of prior lawful residency in another Member State had not been satisfied. The Court of Justice was asked whether the condition of prior lawful residence in another Member State was compatible with Directive 2004/38. The Court of Justice held that the application of the directive was not conditional on the family member having previously resided lawfully in another Member State. The Court said the directive applies to family members who accompany and move with the Union citizen and the definition of family members in the directive does not require lawful residency in another Member State.

In *Ruiz Zambrano v Office national de l'emploi* (Case C–34/09) Mr Zambrano and his wife moved to Belgium as a result of the war in Columbia. The couple sought asylum in Belgium, however they were refused refugee status and they were ordered to leave. While they were residing in Belgium Mr Zambrano's wife gave birth to two children. As a result of their birth in Belgium, the two Zambrano children acquired Belgian nationality. Mr Zambrano brought legal proceedings against the decision of the Belgian authorities that refused his application for residency in Belgium. He argued that as the parent of a minor Belgian national he was entitled to reside and work in Belgium.

A preliminary ruling was sent to the Court of Justice asking if Mr Zambrano could rely on European Union law in order to reside and work in Belgium. The Court of Justice held that under Belgian national law Mr Zambrano's children had acquired Belgian nationality and as a result the children were citizens of the European Union. The court went on to say that by refusing to grant a right of residency to a third-country national who was the parent of dependent minor children, the Zambrano children were being deprived of their rights as Union citizens.

As a result of the *Zambrano* decision a Member State cannot refuse residency to a third-country national who has dependent children with Union citizenship status. A refusal to grant residency to the parents would deprive the children of the genuine enjoyment of the rights that attach to Union citizenship.

LIMITATIONS ON THE GROUNDS OF PUBLIC POLICY, PUBLIC SECURITY OR PUBLIC HEALTH

[12.16] The free movement of persons and citizenship provisions are not absolute and they are subject to certain restrictions. A Member State may restrict the free movement of an individual if there is a breach of public policy, public security or public health.

The Treaty provisions for these limitations are as follows:

- Article 45(3) TFEU relates to workers;
- Article 55 TFEU relates to persons exercising the right of establishment;
- Article 62 TFEU relates to persons providing services.

The Treaty provisions are supplemented by Directive 2004/38. Articles 27 to 33 of Directive 2004/38 elaborates on the provisions of the original directive and consolidates the case law of the Court of Justice of the European Union in the matter.

Public Policy and Public Security

[12.17] Article 27 of Directive 2004/38 states the following:

> 'Measures taken on grounds of public policy or public security shall comply with the principle of proportionality and shall be based exclusively on the personal conduct of the individual concerned. Previous criminal convictions shall not in themselves constitute grounds for taking such measures. The personal conduct of the individual concerned must represent a genuine, present and sufficiently serious threat affecting one of the fundamental interests of society. Justifications that are isolated from the particulars of the case or that rely on considerations or general prevention shall not be accepted.'

The different elements of the definition will now be looked at in turn.

Proportionality

[12.18] Measures that restrict a person's entry and residence must be proportionate to the legitimate aim. If a Member State exercises the right to expel an individual, it must be on grounds that are proportionate to the infringement committed by the individual. An example of this is joined cases *Orfanopoulos and Oliveri* (Cases C–482/01 and C–493/01), [2004] ECR I–5257. *Orfanopoulos* concerned a Greek national who was living in Germany. He was deported from Germany due to a conviction for drug offences. The Court of Justice set out a number of factors that must be considered when deporting an individual from a host state. The factors to be considered are as follows:

1. the seriousness of the offence committed;

2. the length of time that the individual has been residing in the host state;

3.   the length of time the individual has been residing in the host state;

4.   the individuals' family circumstances; and

5.   fundamental rights.

These factors are now contained in Directive 2004/38.

Personal Conduct

[12.19] Member States can bring proceedings for the expulsion of an individual based on the personal conduct of that individual. Personal conduct was considered in the following case of *Van Duyn v Home Office* (Case C–41/74), [1974] ECR 1337.

Van Duyn was a Dutch national who challenged the UK's decision not to allow her entry into the UK for the purpose of working with the Church of Scientology. The UK was of the opinion that the Church of Scientology was socially harmful. Van Duyn argued that membership of the Church of Scientology could not be defined as personal conduct. The court held that it was for the Member State to decide whether or not an individual's conduct was contrary to public policy. The court looked at Van Duyn's association with the Church of Scientology and decided that it could constitute as personal conduct.

In *Criminal proceedings against Donatella Calfa* (Case C–348/96),[1999] ECR I–11 Mr Calfa an Italian national, was convicted of drug offences in Crete. Mr Calfa was sentenced to three months imprisonment and on foot of national legislation he was expelled from Crete for life. The court held that automatic expulsion on foot of a criminal conviction could not be justified. The automatic expulsion rules failed to take account of the personal conduct of the offender or of the danger that person represented. Previous convictions alone are not permitted as a ground for deportation or expulsion.

R v Bouchereau (Case C–30/77), [1977] ECR 1999 considers previous convictions. Bouchereau was a French national living in the

UK and he was found guilty of drug possession. The national court sought to impose a deportation order. However, before the deportation order was put in place a question was sent to the Court of Justice seeking clarification as to whether Boucherau's right to freedom of movement would be infringed. The court considered the previous convictions of the individual and went on to say that previous convictions could only be taken into account when an individual showed a propensity to act in the same way in the future.

A Genuine Present and Sufficiently Serious Threat

[12.20] The individual's conduct must represent a present threat to public policy and security. It is necessary to look at the length of time that has elapsed since the crime was committed and the present threat must be in place at the time of expulsion.

In *Bonsignore v Oberstadtdirektur of the City of Cologne* (Case C–67/74), [1975] ECR 297 it was established that a Member State cannot rely on the public policy and public security limitations for the purpose of general prevention. Bonsignore was an Italian national working in Germany. The German government sought to deport him following a conviction for a firearms offence. The German government said that the deportation was necessary in order to prevent and deter other immigrants from committing similar offences. The Court of Justice rejected the German government's argument. The court said that the decision to deport had to be based on the behaviour of the person convicted of the crime and there must be a present threat to the requirements of public policy. Deportation could not be based on a general preventative reason.

The provisions of the Treaty and the directive prevent Member States from excluding or deporting persons who are exercising their right to move freely under the Treaty provisions. The position is not as clear in relation to restrictions on a person's movement within a host state. *Rutili v Ministre de l'Interior* (Case C–36/75), [1975] ECR 1219 concerned Rutili, an Italian citizen living in France. Rutili was prohibited from entering certain areas in France due to his political involvement. He was a well-known political activist and the

French authorities were of the opinion that he was likely to disturb public policy. The court looked at whether similar restrictions were also placed on French citizens. The court said that the French authorities' actions could only be accepted if similar prohibitions were also placed on French citizens. The restrictions that were being imposed on Mr Rutili were much more severe than those that could be imposed on French nationals and as a result the court said that Mr Rutili's right to free movement throughout France could not be restricted.

[12.21] A different approach was taken in the case of *Ministre d'Interieur v Olazabal,* (Case C–100/01), [2002] ECR I–10981. Olazabal was a Spanish national who had been convicted for terrorism and had served a prison sentence in France. Following his release he was prohibited from residing in certain regions of France close to the Spanish border. The court stated that in situations where nationals of other Member States are liable to be expelled or prohibited during their residency they are equally capable of being subject to less severe measures consisting of partial restrictions on their right of residence. The partial restriction can be justified on grounds of public policy without it being necessary that identical measures are applied by the Member State in question to its own nationals.

Public Health

[12.22] A Member State can only invoke the public health limitations in two situations. According to Art 29 of Directive 2004/ 38 the diseases justifying a restriction on free movement are:

- diseases with epidemic potential; and
- other infectious diseases or contagious parasitic diseases.

If a worker contracts a disease more than three months after entering a country then a Member State cannot use that disease as a ground for expelling the individual.

Chapter 13

Competition Law

INTRODUCTION

[13.01] Competition law ensures that the buying and selling of goods within the European Union is protected from manipulation and as a result competition law plays a pivotal role within the European framework.

Competition law is the tool used by the European Union to ensure that companies operate fairly within the 28 Member States. For example the free movement of goods is one of the primary aims of the European Union and competition law ensures that the free movement of goods is not hindered in any way by the deliberate actions of particular companies.

Competition is the rivalry for business success or optimum sales that exists between companies who operate within the same market. For the purpose of EU law, companies are referred to as undertakings. Competition is essential for success and an undertaking can increase its market strength through competition. A strong market position can be achieved by an undertaking by successfully competing with its competitors. A successful undertaking will hold the highest place on the market and it will constantly compete with other competitors to ensure that this place is maintained on the market.

Undertakings do not always use legitimate methods to compete on the market and as a result competition law is used to monitor market behaviour. Competition law does not prevent or restrict competition but it ensures that there is fair competition between undertakings on the market. The result achieved by competition law is that the market is not negatively affected and trade is not hindered in any way by one undertaking or a group of undertakings.

In order for the aims of the EU Treaties to be achieved it is necessary for the internal market to operate as efficiently as possible.

Competition law is a means of regulating the market and it works in conjunction with the provisions of the Treaties. The EU Treaty articles on Competition Law are Arts 101 and 102 TFEU. These provisions cover two types of anti-competitive activities. Article 101 TFEU deals with restrictive agreements between undertakings that have an anti-competitive object or effect. These agreements are often referred to as cartels. Article 102 TFEU deals with abuse of a dominant position. This occurs where an undertaking uses its position of market strength to prevent other companies from competing on the same market. An undertaking is entitled to enjoy a dominant position. However, an undertaking is not entitled to abuse this dominant position.

[13.02] Competition law began in the USA as a result of the Sherman Act of 1890. In the USA competition law is referred to as anti-trust law due to the fact that the Sherman Act was introduced to deal with anti-competitive practices in the oil and railway industries. The Sherman Act 1890 contained a comprehensive code to remedy the deficit that existed in the common law. Section 1 of the Sherman Act of 1890 states:

> 'Every contract, combination in the form of trust or otherwise, or conspiracy, in restraint of trade or commerce among several states, or with foreign nations is declared to be illegal'.

Section 2 of the Sherman Act 1890 states the following:

> 'Every person who shall monopolize, or attempt to monopolize, or combine or conspire with any other person or persons, to monopolize any part of the trade or commerce among the several States, or with foreign nations, shall be deemed guilty of a felony'.

Article 101 and 102 TFEU represent a European interpretation of ss 1 and 2 of the Sherman Act 1890. However, the EU Treaty provisions on competition law are much more recent than the Sherman Act.

The European Union introduced a competition law regime in 1957 with the Treaty of Rome and competition law in Europe has been steadily developing since its introduction. The Treaty provisions are supplemented by secondary legislation in the form of regulations, directives and decisions. The Commission also issues official notices with guidelines on competition law. The notices from the Commission are not legally binding, however they are important in gaining a better understanding of the Commission's position on different areas of EU law.

In Ireland competition law is governed by the Competition Acts 2002 to 2012. Sections 4 and 5 of the Competition Act 2002 mirror Arts 101 and 102 TFEU. Until 31 October 2014 the Irish Competition Authority monitored competition and ensured the enforcement of competition law in Ireland.

Reform of the Competition Acts has recently taken place in the form of the Competition and Consumer Protection Act 2014. The legislation amalgamates the National Consumer Agency and the Competition Authority in order to improve and enhance both competition law and consumer protection. The Act creates the Competition and Consumer Protection Commission, the new authority responsible for competition enforcement and consumer protection in Ireland.

ARTICLE 101 TFEU

[13.03] Article 101 TFEU applies to scenarios where undertakings enter agreements with each other to act unanimously in order to defeat any competition that exists between them. Price-fixing or market sharing are examples of such agreements. The result of these agreements is that the undertakings who participate can operate independently of any market competition that would otherwise exist. In addition to negatively affecting non-participating undertakings who are competing on the same market, these agreements also negatively affect consumers.

Article 101 TFEU prohibits all agreements between undertakings, decisions by associations of undertakings and concerted practices which may affect trade between Member States and which have as their objective or effect the prevention, restriction or distortion of competition within the common market.

Article 101(1) TFEU provides a non-exhausted list of prohibited agreements. The list of behaviours that constitute prohibited agreements are as follows:

a)   Directly or indirectly fix purchase or selling prices or any other trading conditions.

b)   Limit or control production, markets, technical development or investment.

c)   Share markets or source of supply.

d)   Apply dissimilar conditions to equivalent transactions with other trading parties, thereby placing them at a competitive disadvantage.

e)   Make the conclusion of contracts subject to acceptance by other parties of supplementary obligations which by their nature or according to commercial usage have no connection with the subject of the contracts.

Article 101 offences are categorised as either 'hard core offences' or 'non-hard core offences'. Section 6(2) of the Competition Act defines hardcore offences as price fixing, limiting output or sales or sharing markets or customers. Non-hardcore offences include resale price maintenance or non-compete clauses. Enforcement and penalties will be considered in more detail at the end of this chapter.

Article 101(2) provides that any agreement or decision which comes within Art 101(1) is automatically void. However, Art 101(3) goes on to make provision for exemptions. As a result Art 101(1) will be declared not to apply to an agreement, decision or concerted practice if certain conditions are met. Consequently, a two-stage approach is applied to Art 101:

1.   Does the agreement breach competition law?

2.   Is the breach exempted as a result of its pro-competitive effects. The exemptions will be discussed later in this chapter.

ANTI-COMPETITIVE AGREEMENTS

[13.04] Article 101(1) can be broken down into three components. All three of the following conditions must be satisfied in order for a breach of Art 101 to occur.

1.   Agreement between undertakings, decisions by associations of undertakings and concerted practices;

2.   Which may affect trade between Member States;

3.   Which have as their object or effect the prevention, restriction or distortion of competition within the internal market.

The various components of Art 101(1) will now be looked at in turn.

Agreements

[13.05] An agreement can refer to a formal contract and it can also refer to other less formal arrangements. For example an agreement concluded simply by the shaking of a hand. Also in cartel cases agreements are often made in private without any written proof and all parties are bound to keep the secrecy of the cartel. The key feature for the purpose of Art 101 is that a group of undertakings must reach an agreement together as opposed to the unilateral behaviour of a single undertaking.

A cartel normally involves a group of undertakings that meet secretly to discuss business. The undertakings do not have to be part of the same business group. In fact, the undertakings that form part of a cartel are often undertakings that are in direct competition with each other. The cartel members meet in secret and they discuss prices and they exchange valuable commercial information. Due to the secretive nature of cartels their activity can often be sustained over a long period of time. The result of cartel activity severely restricts competition. The consumer is also adversely affected by the operation of a cartel. The Commission has increased efforts to stop all cartel activity due to the serious adverse effects on both the market and the consumer.

Article 101(1) applies to both vertical and horizontal agreements. Agreements conducted between undertakings that operate on the same market level are horizontal agreements, ie an agreement between two manufacturers. An agreement between undertakings at different market levels are said to be vertical agreements, ie franchising or agency agreements.

Undertakings

[13.06] The Treaties do not contain a definition of 'undertaking'. The term has been interpreted broadly and can include any natural or legal person engaged in commercial activity for the provision of goods or services. As a result companies, partnerships and sole traders are all considered to be undertakings. This broad definition was articulated in *Höfner and Elsner v Macrotron GmbH* (Case C–41/90), [1991] ECR I–1979, [1993] 4 CMLR 306, where the court stated;

> 'The concept of an undertaking encompasses every entity engaged in an economic activity regardless of the legal status of the entity and the way in which it is financed.'

However, it should be noted that employees are not undertakings for the purpose of this definition.

Decisions

[13.07] A decision can require associations of undertakings to engage in a particular type of behaviour. Decisions often apply to a group of undertakings engaged in a similar economic activity or trade associations. Trade associations occur when a group of undertakings are involved in the same business activities and they form a group based on that affiliation.

Associations sometimes coordinate the activities of their members without an actual agreement taking place, ie there is a decision made on behalf of the association of undertakings. The coordination of activities by associations can often result in an anti-competitive effect. As a result, the concept of 'decisions' was incorporated into Art 101(1).

Concerted Practices

[13.08] A concerted practice occurs where a group of undertakings engage in some form of similar behaviour that restricts competition. The concept is difficult to define as it normally occurs even where an informal oral agreement has not taken place. The definition can cover any kind of collusion between the undertakings or even a consensus or understanding that the undertakings will not compete with each other.

The Court of Justice provided a definition for a concerted practice in *Imperial Chemical Industries Ltd v Commission* ('*Dyestuffs*' case) (Case C–48/69) [1972] ECR 619, [1972] CMLR 557. In this case the court held that a concerted practice is;

> 'A form of coordination between undertakings which, without having reached the stage where an agreement properly so called has been concluded, knowingly substitutes practical cooperation between them for the risks of competition.'

The definition was extended in *Suiker Unie v Commission* (Cases C–40–48, 50, 54–56, 111, 113, 114/73), [1975] ECR 1663, [1976] 1 CMLR 295 where the court considered whether it was necessary for the undertakings to have an actual plan in place in order to meet the concerted practice requirements. The court held that it was not necessary to have a plan in place and that it was sufficient to have any direct or indirect contact between the undertakings. Once the result of the actions influence the market it is not necessary for the undertakings to be participating in a formal plan of cooperation.

In *Huls AG v Commission (Polypropylene)* (Case C–199/92), the court considered the definition of a concerted practice further and stated that in addition to the concerted practice taking place, there must be subsequent conduct on the market and a relationship of cause and effect between the two. However the court went on to say that a concerted practice would come within the terms of Art 101 even if there were no anti-competitive effects on the market.

[13.09] There is a presumption that the undertakings participating in the concerted practice have access to information exchanged with their competitors and that they use this information for the purpose of determining their conduct on the market. As a result there is an onus on the undertakings participating in the concerted practice to rebut this presumption or prove that the contrary is in fact true.

Consequently, when the Commission establishes that a concerted practice has taken place or is ongoing the burden of proof shifts from the Commission to the undertakings. The undertakings must then prove that there was no conduct on the market as the presumption is that if there was conduct on the market it would be unavoidable to not take into account the information exchanged with their competitors.

The causal link between concerted practice and market conduct was confirmed by the Court of Justice in *T-Mobile Netherlands BV v Raad van Bestuur van de Netherlandse Mededingingsautoriteit* (Case C–8/08), [2009] ECR I–4529, 5 CMLR 11.

Effect on Trade

[13.10] A breach of Art 101(1) will not occur unless the agreement, decision or concerted practice affects trade between Member States.

The Court of Justice has adopted a broad interpretation of what constitutes an effect on trade between Member States pursuant to Art 101(1). To help with interpretation the Commission has provided guidance on the effect on trade between Member States in its notice: Guidelines on the effect on trade concept contained in Articles 81 and 82 [now 101 and 102] of the Treaty [Official Journal C 101 of 27.4.2004]

According to the guidelines the analysis of the concept of 'affecting trade' requires three aspects to be addressed. The following is an extract from the Commission's Notice.

'The concept of "trade between EU countries": the concept of "trade" is not limited to traditional exchanges of goods and services across borders. It is a wider concept, covering all cross-border economic activity including establishment. This interpretation is consistent with the fundamental objective of the Treaty to promote free movement of goods, services, persons and capital. The requirement that there must be an effect on trade "between EU countries" implies that there must be an impact on cross-border economic activity involving at least two EU countries;

The notion "may affect": the function of the notion "may affect" is to define the nature of the required impact on trade between EU countries. According to the standard test developed by the Court of Justice, the notion "may affect" implies that it must be possible to foresee with a sufficient degree of probability on the basis of a set of objective factors of law or fact that the agreement or practice may have an influence, direct or indirect, actual or potential, on the pattern of trade between EU countries. In cases where the agreement or practice is liable to affect the competitive structure inside the EU, EU law jurisdiction is established;

The concept of "appreciability": the effect on trade criterion incorporates a quantitative element, limiting EU law jurisdiction to agreements and practices that are capable of having effects of a certain magnitude. Appreciability can be appraised in particular by reference to the position and the importance of the relevant undertakings on the market for the products concerned. The assessment of appreciability depends on the circumstances of each individual case, in particular the nature of the agreement and practice, the nature of the products covered and the market position of the undertakings concerned'.

OBJECT OR EFFECT

[13.11] Article 101(1) prohibits any agreement, decision or concerted practices between undertakings which have as their object or effect the prevention, restriction or distortion of competition. In order to satisfy this requirement there must be a direct or indirect effect or the capability of such an effect. This is a very broad definition and once any of the requirements are met an abuse has occurred. It is not necessary to satisfy all the requirements. For example an infringement of Art 101(1) will still have occurred even if a cartel was not a success it is sufficient to show that the cartel had the object of hindering competition.

Object

[13.12] If the object of an agreement deliberately restricts competition, Art 101(1) will automatically apply even if the agreement does not have the effect of restricting competition. The word object relates to the aim of the agreement. In *Consten and Grundig v Commission* (Joined Cases C–56 and 58/64), [1966] ECR 299, [1966] CMLR 418 the court considered the meaning of 'object' in relation to the prevention, restriction or distortion of competition. In this case a new type of electrical equipment was introduced to France. The overall effect of the agreement between the suppliers and distributors actually increased inter-brand competition. As this was the result, the question the court had to consider was whether the agreement had through its object or effect restricted, prevented or distorted competition. The agreement between the parties gave absolute territorial protection to Consten and this distorted competition. Once an agreement has the 'object' of preventing, restricting or distorting competition it is caught by Art 101(1) and there is no subsequent requirement to analyse and establish the 'effect' of the agreement.

Effect

[13.13] The effect of an agreement is easier to define. If an agreement does not set out to restrict competition but does so in reality, then Art 101(1) will apply to the agreement. Therefore, intent is not necessary all that is required is that the agreement is anti-competitive in practice.

In *Société Technique Minière v Maschinenbau* (Case C–56/65) [1966] ECR 235, [1966] 1 CMLR 565 the court considered an agreement concerning exclusive distribution. In this case there was no absolute territorial protection as there was in *Consten and Grundig* however the agreement provided for the supplier not to appoint another distributor or to sell the goods itself. The court acknowledged the benefits to competition that such agreements can have. The court then went on to look at the effect on competition in comparison with the effect on competition if the agreement had not been implemented. The Court said:

'it may be doubted whether there is an interference with competition if the said agreement seems really necessary for the penetration of a new area by an undertaking'.

This is a clear example of the court utilising the positive and negative impact of the agreement on competition in its analysis of an Art 101 infringement as opposed to engaging in an Art 101(3) analysis.

Prevention, Restriction or Distortion of Competition

[13.14] The terms 'prevention, restriction or distortion' are used interchangeably and each term has equal and equivalent meaning. Examples of the 'prevention, restriction or distortion of competition' include the offences as contained in Art 101(1) such as fixing purchase or selling prices, limiting or controlling production, markets, technical development or investment, sharing markets or sources or supply, discriminatory prices, or tying arrangements.

The *De Minimus* Doctrine

[13.15] In order for an agreement to be caught by the terms of Art 101(1) it must have an 'appreciable' effect on competition. This principle of an agreement having an 'appreciable' effect is known as the *de minimus* doctrine.

The *de minimus* doctrine was first articulated by the court in *Volk v Vervaecke* (Case C–5/69), [1969] ECR 295, [1969] CMLR 273. Here the court stated that if an agreement has an insignificant effect on the market it will not be in breach of Art 101(1).

The Commission has also issued guidelines on agreements that will not contravene the Art 101(1) criteria in its Notice on Agreements of Minor Importance [2001] C 368/07. The Commission Notice on the *de minimus* doctrine states that for horizontal agreements the market share held by the parties to the agreement cannot exceed 10 per cent of the relevant market. For vertical agreements the market share held by the parties to the agreement cannot exceed 15 per cent. In situations where it cannot be ascertained whether the agreement is vertical or horizontal, a 10 per cent threshold will apply.

Effect on Inter-State Trade

[13.16] The agreement must affect trade between the Member States in order to contravene Art 101(1) if the agreement does not affect trade between the Member States then the national Member States competition law rules apply.

The court outlined a test for assessing whether an agreement affects inter-state trade in *Societe Technique Miniere v Maschinenbau* (Case C–56/65), [1966] ECR 235, [1966] 1 CMLR 565. The test is broad and states,

> 'It must be possible to forsee with a sufficient degree of probability on the basis of a set of objective factors of law or fact that the agreement in question may have an influence, direct or indirect, actual or potential, on the pattern of trade between Member States'

The Commission has provided an interpretation on what constitutes an effect on trade in its Notice, Guidelines on the Effect of Trade contained in Arts 81 and 82 [now Arts 101 and 102] of the Treaty [2004] OJ C 101/81. In essence the purpose of the analysis is to decide whether the infringement falls within the jurisdiction of the European Court or the jurisdiction of the relevant national court.

ARTICLE 101(3) EXEMPTIONS

[13.17] Article 101(3) TFEU provides the Commission and the Competition Authority with the power to exempt agreements that are infringing Art 101(1). The exemption can only be granted when the conditions set out in Art 101(3) are met.

The Art 101(3) conditions are as follows:

An agreement, decision or concerted practice must:

a)   contribute to improving the production or distribution of goods or to promoting technical or economic progress; and

b)   allow consumers a fair share of the resulting benefits.

An agreement, decision or concerted practice must not:

1.   impose on the undertakings concerned restrictions which are not indispensible to the attainment of these objectives; and

2.   afford such undertakings, the possibility of eliminating competition in respect of a substantial part of the products in question.

AUTOMATIC EXEMPTIONS

[13.18] Council Regulation (EC) 1/2003 came into force in 2004 and it changed the enforcement mechanism of competition law. Prior to 2004 the Commission held the exclusive power to grant exemptions however the regulation decentralised enforcement to national competition authorities in the Member States. Council Regulation (EC) 1/2003 provides that agreements that come within

Art 101(1) are not in breach of EU competition law if the conditions of Art 101(3) are satisfied. In order to be guaranteed this exemption the agreement must meet all the conditions set out in Art 101(3).

Prior to the coming into force of the regulation in 2004, exemptions had to be sought from the Commission pursuant to a notification procedure. The regulation has abolished the notification procedure and undertakings are now responsible for ensuring whether or not the agreement is in breach of Art 101(1) and whether a subsequent exemption applies under Art 101(3).

The Commission has issued a five-year report and a ten-year communication on the operation of Council Regulation (EC) 1/2003. The reports from the Commission on the effectiveness of the regulation state that it is has positively contributed to the stronger enforcement of EU competition rules.

BLOCK EXEMPTIONS

[13.19] Block exemptions allow categories of agreements to be exempted from the provisions of Art 101(1). The Commission issues block exemptions in the form of regulations. The regulation sets out criteria and once these are satisfied the agreement is exempt. As with the automatic exemptions it is the responsibility of those seeking to rely on the block exemption to ensure compliance with the criteria. Block exemptions provide class relief in broad areas of agreements that include:

- Commission Regulation (EU) 1218/2010 which concerns specialisation agreements;

- Commission Regulation (EU) 1217/2010 which concerns research and development agreements; and

- Commission Regulation (EU) 330/2010 which concerns vertical agreements including franchising agreements, exclusive distributions agreements and exclusive purchasing agreements.

ARTICLE 102 TFEU

[13.20] Article 102 TFEU prohibits a dominant undertaking from engaging in abusive practices that affect the internal market of the European Union.

The prohibited behaviour contained in Art 102 TFEU is as follows:

'Any abuse by one or more undertakings of a dominant position within the common market or in a substantial part of it shall be prohibited as incompatible with the internal market in so far as it may affect trade between Member States

Such abuse may, in particular, consist in:

(a) directly or indirectly imposing unfair purchase or selling prices or other unfair trading conditions;

(b) limiting production, markets or technical development to the prejudice of consumers;

(c) applying dissimilar conditions to equivalent transactions with other trading parties, thereby placing them at a competitive disadvantage;

(d) making the conclusion of contracts subject to acceptance by the other parties of supplementary obligations which, by their nature or according to commercial usage, have no connection with the subject of such contracts.'

It is <u>not</u> anti-competitive <u>to hold a dominant position</u> on the market but it is anti-competitive if an undertaking uses that dominant position to engage in anti-competitive practices that affect the internal market.

Article 102 TFEU contains three requirements and if these three requirements are all satisfied an infringement will occur. The three requirements are as follows:

- the undertaking must hold a dominant position in the relevant market;

- the undertaking must have abused its dominant position; and

- the abuse must have affected trade within the European Union.

Investigating an infringement of Art 102 involves detailed analysis of all <u>three</u> requirements.

DOMINANT POSITION

[13.21] A definition of a dominant position was provided by the Court of Justice in *United Brands v Commission* (Case C–27/76), [1978] ECR 207:

> 'A position of economic strength enjoyed by an undertaking which enables it to prevent effective competition being maintained on the relevant market by giving it the power to behave to an appreciable extent independently of its competitors, customers and ultimately of it consumers'

Article 102 TFEU only applies to undertakings that hold a dominant position and there is no breach of Art 102 TFEU if dominance is not established. Determining whether or not an undertaking holds a dominant position is the starting point for an Art 102 TFEU investigation.

When considering whether or not an undertaking is dominant it is necessary to observe the relevant market where the undertaking carries on business. The relevant market is divided into three categories:

- relevant product market;
- relevant geographic market; and
- relevant temporal market.

An undertaking is less likely to be dominant in a wide market because its market share will be smaller. Therefore an undertaking that is under scrutiny will attempt to establish the widest possible relevant market. The Commission will attempt to establish a narrow relevant market because an undertaking is more likely to be dominant as a result of holding a larger market share on a smaller relevant market.

RELEVANT PRODUCT MARKET

[13.22] The relevant product market is made up of the particular product in question and similar products that are considered to be substitutes. The Commission has defined the relevant product market as follows:

> 'A relevant product market comprises all those products and/ or services which are regarded as interchangeable or substitutable by the consumer by reason of the products' characteristics, their prices and their intended use'.

The central issue when defining the relevant product market is product interchangeability or substitutability.

Interchangeability is assessed under two headings:

1.   Demand-side interchangeability
2.   Supply-side interchangeability

Demand-side Interchangeability

[13.23] Demand-side interchangeability relates to consumer behaviour. When assessing demand-side interchangeability it is necessary to consider will the consumer substitute one product for another or will the consumer readily switch between products. If the consumer substitutes or switches between products then the products are interchangeable. All products that are interchangeable form the relevant product market.

Product pricing is also used as a means of testing consumer behaviour. In 1997, the Commission put forward a test in the Notice on the Definition of the Relevant Market. The test is based on consumer response to a small but significant product price increase. If the consumer switches to another product in response to a small but permanent price increase (normally between 5 per cent and 10 per cent) then this shows the products are interchangeable. If the consumer does not switch to another product then the product is in a separate market. This test is also known as the SSNIP test (small but significant non-transitory increase in price).

In *United Brands v Commission* (Case C–27/76), [1978] ECR 207 the Court of Justice considered the relevant product market. The issue was:

1.   Did bananas form part of the fresh fruit market? or
2.   Did bananas form a separate and distinct market?

If bananas were interchangeable with other fresh fruits they would form part of the fresh fruit market. However, the Court of Justice held that bananas were a separate and distinct market. The rationale for the decision was that the banana had special characteristics and as a result it was not interchangeable with other fresh fruit. The court went on to say that because of the appearance, taste, softness, seedlessness and easy handling of bananas they were particularly suitable for the old, sick and very young, making them separate and distinct from other fresh fruit.

Supply-side Interchangeability

[13.24] Supply-side interchangeability relates to the behaviour of producers that supply similar products. When assessing supply-side interchangeability it is necessary to consider whether a producer can easily change their production methods in order to produce a similar product. If it is easily achievable and cost effective for a producer to enter a similar product market then there is supply side interchangeability. All products that are interchangeable in this way form part of the relevant product market.

Relevant Geographic Market

[13.25] The relevant geographic market is the area where the conditions of competition are the same for all traders. The Commission has defined the relevant geographic market as follows.

> 'The relevant geographic market comprises that area in which the undertaking concerned are involved in the supply and demand of products or services in which the conditions

of competition are sufficiently homogenous and which can
be distinguished from neighbouring areas because the
conditions of competition are appreciably different in those
areas.'

When defining the relevant geographic market, it is necessary to
look at how a product is supplied throughout the European Union. If
a product is supplied easily throughout the European Union then
there is a broad geographic market. However, if the cost of
transportation is very high and if it is difficult to supply a product
throughout the European Union then the geographic area is said to
be narrow.

In *Italian Flatglass* (Case T–68, 77 and 78/89), [1992] ECR II–1403
the Commission focused on geographic location and the
transportation of goods. The Commission stated that the greater the
distance between the production plant and the supply point the more
difficult it would be to transport a product and as a result a
producer's competitiveness would be reduced. As a result of that
reasoning, the Commission decided that the relevant geographic
market in *Italian Flatglass* was Italy. However, this decision was
overturned in the Court of First Instance on appeal where it was held
that the Commission had not properly assessed the market. The
court went on to say that the Commission should have also examined
products from other countries and looked at the distance between
production plants and supply points in these countries.

In *Hilti v Commission* (Case T–30/89), [1991] ECR II–1439, the
Commission found that the relevant geographic market does not
have to be contained in the geographic area of just of one Member
State. In *Hilti* the market for nail cartridges was found to be the
entire European Union. The reason for this decision was that nail
cartridges could be transported around the European Union easily
and at a relatively low cost.

Relevant Temporal Market

[13.26] The relevant temporal market only applies to certain cases.
The relevant product market and the relevant geographic market will

always form part of an Art 102 analysis, however the relevant temporal market will not always feature in this analysis.

The relevant temporal market relates to the seasonal market of a product and not all products are affected by the seasons. For example, fresh fruit will be affected by a temporal market. During the summer months fresh fruit is abundant but during the winter months it is not as easily obtained. As a result the competitive conditions in the fresh fruit market will vary from season to season.

The temporal market was examined in the case of *United Brands*. In this case evidence was put forward to show that during the summer months demand for bananas dropped as there was an abundance of other fresh fruit available. However, in the winter when other fresh fruit was not available the demand for bananas increased. Therefore, the banana market could be divided into two temporal markets. This argument was rejected by the Commission and instead it based its decision on just one temporal market due to the fact that the ripening of bananas takes place the whole year round.

DOMINANCE

[13.27] Once the relevant product and geographic market has been identified the next step is to determine whether the undertaking is dominant on the relevant market.

When assessing whether or not an undertaking is dominant it is necessary to look at the market share and the market power held by an undertaking. The market share and the market power are said to be the main indicators of dominance.

MARKET SHARE

[13.28] In reality it is very rare for a company to have a 100 per cent market share. Careful analysis of the market is necessary in order to assess if an undertaking is in a dominant position. The Commission has issued guidance on assessing market shares for this purpose and it states that an undertaking is unlikely to hold a dominant position if its market share is below 40 per cent.

In *Michelin v Commission* (Case 322/81), [1983] ECR 3461 a market share of 57 per cent to 65 per cent was held to amount to a dominant position. In this case the next nearest competitor also had a much smaller market share. Another factor taken into account in *Michelin* was that it would take another undertaking 25 years to set up a company with a similar situation as Michelin and this pointed to the fact that Michelin had held a dominant position for quite a long time.

In *AKZO Chemie BV v Commission* (Case C–62/86), [1991] ECR I–3359, the court held that a market share of 50 per cent or higher would usually give rise to a position of dominance.

In *United Brands* the undertaking held a 40 to 45 per cent share of the market. The court took other factors into account and as a result the undertaking was held to be dominant. One of the other factors taken into account was the fact that United Brands sold twice as much as its nearest competitor.

ADDITIONAL FACTORS

[13.29] Market shares are not the only indicators of dominance to be considered and the court will often look at a variety of other factors to establish dominance.

Access to Capital

[13.30] If an undertaking has access to substantial financial resources this may allow the undertaking to maintain a strong market position. For example an undertaking with extensive financial resources will be able to engage in consistent price cutting and selling below cost in a way that a small undertaking could not compete with. An undertaking can also use its financial resources to engage in product development or an undertaking can also use financial resources to engage in world wide advertising.

Intellectual Property Rights

[13.31] The possession of intellectual property rights can also be an indicator of dominance. An undertaking can use intellectual property rights to prevent competitors from gaining any hold within the market.

Vertical Integration

[13.32] If an undertaking has vertical integration it is said to control both the production and supply chain. In the *United Brands* case the court stated that United Brands was vertically integrated to a very high degree. This was demonstrated by the fact that United Brands was the owner of plantations, the controller of loading operations, it had a vast transportation system and it controlled distributors and wholesalers throughout the world.

ABUSE OF A DOMINANT POSITION

[13.33] It is not anti-competitive to hold a dominant position on the market. It is anti-competitive if an undertaking uses that dominant position to engage in anti-competitive practices that affect the internal market. In order to assess whether or not a company is abusing a dominant position it is necessary to first consider whether the company holds a dominant position on the relevant market and then to see if that position is being abused.

Once it has been established that an undertaking is dominant on a particular market the next step is to assess whether or not that undertaking has engaged in one of the accepted types of abuse. The types of abuse are as follows:

- directly or indirectly imposing unfair purchase or selling prices or other unfair trading conditions;

- limiting production markets or technical developments to the prejudice of consumers;

- applying dissimilar conditions to equivalent transactions with other trading parties thereby placing them at a competitive disadvantage;

- making the conclusion of contracts subject to acceptance by the other parties of supplementary obligations which, by their very nature or according to commercial usage, have no connection with the subject of such contracts.

This is not an exhaustive list and it simply gives examples of types of abusive behaviour.

The types of abuse are often divided into two sub categories of abuse. The two categories are exploitative and anti-competitive abuses. Exploitative abuses exploit the consumer and anti-competitive abuses restrict competition for other undertakings. In reality most kinds of abuse are both exploitative and anti-competitive.

Refusal to Supply

[13.34] This example of an abuse was established in *Commercial Solvents* (Case 6 & 7/73), [1974] ECR 223. In this case commercial solvents refused to supply raw material. The Court held that an undertaking cannot cut off supplies to a former customer in order to compete in the former customer's market.

In *RTE & ITP v Commission* (Case C–241&242/91 P) [1995] ECR I–743 the court held that the refusal to supply intellectual property rights can amount to the abuse of a dominant position. This case concerned the publication of TV listings owned by RTE, ITV and BBC Northern Ireland. The three companies made a profit from royalties through selling their TV listings to newspapers. Magill wanted to make a consolidated weekly TV guide, however the three companies refused to make the copyrighted material available to Magill. The court and the Commission looked at the position of the consumer and both agreed that the consumer would benefit from a consolidated weekly TV guide. The court held that it was an abuse of a dominant position if a copyright holder prevented a third party from introducing a new product that would be superior to the existing product of the dominant undertaking.

However, in *Oscar Bronner* (Case C–7/97) a media company's refusal to supply a daily newspaper through a home delivery service did not amount to an abuse of Art 102. The court stated that the refusal to supply did not prevent the company from setting up its own nationwide home delivery paper service.

Essential Facilities

[13.35] This occurs where a company controls an essential facility and other companies are not able to compete without access to this facility. A breach of Art 102 will occur if the dominant company refuses access to the essential facility. This occurred in the Commission decision of *Sealink/B&I-Holyhead Interim Measures* [1992] 5 CMLR 255.

In this case Sealink was the owner of Holyhead Port and it operated a ferry service in and out of Holyhead Port. B&I and Sealink were competitors however Sealink had an obligation to open its port to competitors and it did so. B&I contended that Sealink had opened the port in an unfair manner. B&I claimed that the loading and unloading of B&I ferries was being interfered with by the sailing times of Sealink ferries. The Commission agreed with B&I and found that the rescheduling of Sealink ferries did place B&I at a competitive disadvantage. Sealink had abused its dominant position by restricting competition in the ferry port.

[13.36] Similarly, in 2004 Microsoft was fined €497m by the Commission for abusing its dominant position in PC operating systems. Microsoft had abused their position by refusing to provide the required interfaces to competitors to enable their products to work with Microsoft Windows Operating System. (Commission Decision 24 March 2004, COMP/C/37792)

Abusive Pricing

[13.37] Abusive pricing occurs when different consumers are offered different prices for the same product. In addition to setting the price too high, unfairly low prices are also prohibited by Art 102. An extremely low price is also referred to as predatory pricing. Predatory pricing occurs where an undertaking trades at prices so low that other competitors are forced out of the market. Once the other competitors are forced out of the market the company in the dominant position usually increases its prices again.

In *AKZO Chemie BV v Commission* (Case C–62/86), [1991] ECR I–3359 initial complaint was made by ECS a small company that sold benzoyl peroxide. ECS claimed that AKZO's predatory pricing strategy was forcing them out of the market. The Commission found that AKZO had abused its dominant position and this was upheld by the court.

Tying

[13.38] Tying occurs where a dominant undertaking refuses to supply one product unless another product is also bought with it. *Hilti v Commission* (Case T–30/89), [1991] ECR II–1439 concerned the manufacture of nail guns. *Hilti* made the supply of cartridges to their retailers conditional on the purchase of nails to use with the cartridges. The Commission found that this was an abuse of Art 102.

Tying also arose in 2004 in the case of *Microsoft* (Commission Decision 24 March 2004, COMP/C/37792). The Commission found that Microsoft had abused its dominant position by 'tying' its Windows Media Player to its Windows Operating System. As a result of the decision Microsoft had to offer customers a Windows Operating System that did not include Windows Media Player.

In March 2013, Microsoft was fined €561m for not offering customers a web browser choice on their computer screens. This was as a result of an investigation launched by the Commission after

Microsoft failed to comply with a commitment decision entered in 2009.

Illegal Rebates

[13.39] Rebates are often offered to customers and are a legitimate means of rewarding customers for their support. However, to be compatible with Art 102 a rebate must be not have the effect of restricting the customers freedom to choose between operators. A rebate that restricts choice is referred to as 'loyalty' or 'fidelity' rebate and this type of rebate is an abuse of a dominant position. In *Hoffman la Roche* (Case 85/76) the court stated that an undertaking would be guilty of an abuse where it adopts a system of fidelity rebates.

In *Intel v Commission* (Case T–286/09) the Commission imposed a fine of €1.06b on Intel for abusing its dominant position on the market for x86 central processing units. Intel granted rebates to four major computer manufactures (Dell, Lenovo, HP and NEC) provided that they purchased almost all of their x86 central processing units from Intel. Intel also awarded payments to Media Saturn which were conditional on it exclusively selling computers containing Intel's x86 central processing units. The Commission stated that the rebates and the payments resulted in loyalty and an inability to compete on the part of Media Saturn and the four major computer manufacturers. The Commission also stated that there was a reduction in consumer choice and there were lower incentives to innovate.

ENFORCEMENT OF COMPETITION LAW

Council Regulation (EC) 1/2003

[13.40] In the area of competition law it is the European Commission who supervises and enforces competition law infringements. In the past only the Commission had responsibility for the enforcement of competition law. This position changed following the enactment of Council Regulation (EC) 1/2003 on December 16, 2002. The regulation which is also known as the Modernisation Regulation decentralised the enforcement of competition law. A national competition law system is now by operated by every Member State in the EU. National competition authorities work alongside the European Commission enforcing competition law and this is known as dual enforcement.

As a result of the Modernisation Regulation the enforcement of Competition Law is shared by the Commission, the national competition authorities and the national courts of the Member States. Competition law enforcement now involves a European-wide competition network where there is open discussion and cooperation. It is the Commission and not the Court of Justice that gives decisions on competition law infringements at European level. The Commission both investigates and prosecutes whilst working with the national competition authorities. An appeal against the Commission's decision can be brought to the General Court.

The Commission focuses on major cases of significance from a competition and European perspective and the national competition authorities work on smaller cases.

National competition authorities operate in the 28 Member States and they apply both national competition law and EU competition law to an infringement of competition law within the Member State. Pursuant to Council Regulation (EC) 1/2003 there is a duty of cooperation between the national competition authorities. The Commission has issued a notice on how this cooperation is to operate. Pursuant to this notice competition law cases can be allocated in three different ways:

- A single national competition authority is usually well placed to deal with agreements or practices that substantially affect competition mainly within its territory. A single competition authority will deal with a case if it has effect on competition within its territory and if it can effectively bring the infringement to an end and it can gather evidence without the assistance of third parties.

- Action by two or three national competition authorities will be appropriate where an agreement or practice has a substantial effect on competition mainly in their respective territories and the action of only one national competition authority would not be sufficient to bring the entire infringement to an end.

- The Commission will deal with cases where more than three Member States' territories are involved.

Pursuant to Art 23(2) of Council Regulation (EC) 1/2003, the Commission can fine an undertaking up to 10 per cent of its turnover in all products worldwide in the preceding year for substantive breaches of Art 101 and 102. The Commission can also impose fines of up to 1 per cent of an undertaking's turnover in the preceding year where an undertaking supplies false information under Art 17 and 18 of Council Regulation (EC) 1/2003 or does not cooperate with inspections under Art 23(1) of the regulation.

Article 24 of Council Regulation (EC) 1/2003 provides for periodic penalty payments which cannot exceed 5 per cent of an undertaking's daily turnover in the preceding year. These payments apply where an undertaking continues to infringe the competition provisions and continually fails to comply with an interim decision or commitment or continually fails to provide complete and correct information to the Commission on request.

Leniency

[13.41] Leniency only applies in relation to Art 101 and cartel cases where an undertaking is the first to inform the Commission about a cartel. The Commission adopted its first Leniency Notice in 1996, which was subsequently revised in 2002 and once again in 2006 with the Notice on immunity from fines and reduction of fines in cartel cases.

If an undertaking is the first to inform the Commission it will be granted full immunity from any fine that would otherwise be imposed on it for its participation in the cartel. The undertaking must cooperate fully and it must provide all necessary information. It must end its participation in the cartel and most importantly it must not have been the ringleader, otherwise it will not receive immunity.

An example of the Leniency Programme in action occurred in 2002 in a case concerning two auction houses in London. Christie's and Sotheby's had participated in a price fixing cartel. Christie's gave the Commission information and as a result they were granted immunity from fines. The Commission had no investigation open when they received the information from Christie's. The information received provided 'decisive proof' of a cartel and as a result Christie's received full immunity from fines. The requirement for 'decisive proof' has been subsequently removed in order to encourage company participation in the Leniency Programme.

Irish Legislation

[13.42] In Ireland the Competition Acts 2002–2012 deal with anti-competitive behaviour. Ireland is unique in that it also has criminal sanctions in addition to civil remedies for breaches of competition law. Section 4 of the Competition Act relates to Art 101 and provides the following sanctions:

- On summary conviction there is a fine not exceeding €5,000. In the case of an individual there can be a fine or imprisonment for a term not exceeding six months or a fine and imprisonment.

- On indictment there can be a fine not exceeding whichever of the following amounts is greater, €5m, or 10 per cent of the turnover of the undertaking in the financial year ending in the twelve months period prior to conviction. For individuals there is the same fine but a term of imprisonment not exceeding ten years or to both fine and imprisonment.

Section 5 of the Competition Act covers abuse of a dominant position contained in Article 102. The Competition Act 2002 makes it a criminal offence to breach Article 102 and the sanctions are as follows;

- On summary conviction the fine is €5,000. The daily fine for a continuing contravention is €500.

- On indictment the fine is €5m or 10 per cent of the turnover. The daily fine for a continuing contravention is €50,000. For breaches under s 5 individuals can be fined but not imprisoned.

The Competition Act 2012 introduced a number of changes to civil enforcement of competition law in Ireland.

- The Probation Act will no longer apply to competition offences.

- The Competition Authority (now the Competition and Consumer Protection Commission) has been given the power to accept commitments from those under investigation for competition law breaches. The commitment can then be made an order of court by the High Court. Failure to comply with the commitment will result in contempt of court.

- When an Irish court has found that an undertaking has breached competition law any person who has suffered as a result of that breach may take a 'follow-on' action. In addition to being permitted to take a 'follow-on' action the plaintiff will be further assisted by the fact that the court finding of a competition law infringement will be *res judicata*. This means that the plaintiff in a 'follow-on' action will not be required to prove that a breach of competition law has occurred only that they suffered harm.

The Competition and Consumer Protection Act 2014 improves the enforcement of competition law by increasing the powers available to the Competition and Consumer Protection Commission. For example, the power to compel the disclosure of material that may be legally privileged and the power to order the disclosure of Internet and call data. This will ensure better investigation and prosecution of competition law infringements.

PRIVATE ACTIONS FOR DAMAGES UNDER EU COMPETITION LAW

[13.43] Victims of competition law infringements are entitled to bring a claim for compensation in their national courts. However, despite the improvements in this area such as those brought about by the Competition Act 2012 in Ireland the legal frameworks in many Member States makes the process difficult and costly for the victims of infringements.

In order to remedy this situation the Commission put forward a proposal for a directive to facilitate damages claims by victims of competition law violations. The directive will provide for private enforcement of competition law which is a legal action brought by a private individual. Public enforcement of competition law will still be carried out by the Commission and the competition authorities. It is envisaged that both public and private enforcement will complement each other rather than replace each other and that a more effective competition enforcement strategy will be achieved.

The directive puts forward a number of important tools to help the victims of competition law infringements:

- Parties will have easier access to evidence.

- Claimants will be able to rely on a national competition authority's finding of an infringement.

- There will be clarification on limitation periods for victims.

- Victims have the right to compensation for actual loss and loss of profit plus interest from the time the harm occurred until compensation is paid.

- Out of court resolution is facilitated in order to achieve compensation faster at less cost.

The European Parliament and the Council agreed the text of the directive during the ordinary legislative procedure in April 2014. The Parliament adopted a draft text of the directive on 21 October 2014 and a similar action is expected from the Council. Following on from this, the directive will be signed into law and published in the official journal. Member States will then have two years to implement the directive into their national legal systems.

Chapter 14

State Aid

INTRODUCTION

[14.01] The operation of state aid within a particular Member State can affect the market and as a result state aid and how it operates is monitored by competition law. State aid is when a public authority gives aid to a particular undertaking in an attempt to give that undertaking an advantage. Articles 107–109 TFEU regulate state aid. Article 107(1) TFEU contains the prohibition on state aid and it provides;

> 'save as otherwise provided in the Treaties any aid granted by a Member State or through state resources in any form whatsoever which distorts or threatens to distort competition by favouring certain undertakings or the production of certain goods shall, insofar as it affects trade between Member States be incompatible with the internal market'.

Article 107 contains four requirements that must be present in order for an action to be deemed state aid. For a Member States actions to be considered state aid the following must have occurred:

1. The action must confer an advantage
2. The aid must be provided by state resources;
3. There must be distortion or a threat of distortion of competition law;
4. There must be an effect on inter-state trade.

The court consider these requirements in *France v Commission (Stardust Marine)* (Case C–482/99), [2002] ECR I–4397 and *Phillip Morris Holland BV v Commission* (Case 730/79), [1980] ECR I–2671 and *Italy v the Commission*, (Case 173/73), [1974] ECR 709.

MEANING OF 'STATE'

[14.02] The court has interpreted the meaning of 'state' for the purposes of Art 107 TFEU very broadly. As a result 'state' has been held to include regional or local authorities, public authorities and public bodies. The meaning of 'state resources' has also been interpreted broadly.

AID MUST BE GRANTED BY MEMBER STATE

[14.03] The Treaty provisions do not provide a definition of state aid and as a result the European Court of Justice and the Commission have provided guidance on the definition. The Commission has provided a non-exhaustive list of what it considers to be state aid. The list is as follows:

a)   tax exemptions;

b)   direct subsidies;

c)   exemptions from prior fiscal charges;

d)   preferential interest rates;

e)   favourable loan guarantees;

f)   provision of land or buildings on preferential terms;

g)   indemnities against losses;

h)   deferment of the collection of fiscal or social contributions;

i)   dividend guarantees.

The definition of 'state aid' was considered in *Altmark* (Case C–280/00). In this case the Court of Justice held that financial support that amounts to public service compensation was not state aid once certain conditions were satisfied. The court stated that four conditions must be satisfied in order for public service compensation **not** to be classified as state aid. The conditions are as follows:

1.   The recipient undertaking must actually have public service obligations to discharge and those obligations must be clearly defined.

2.   The parameters on the basis of which the compensation is calculated must be established in advance in an objective and transparent manner.

3.   The compensation cannot exceed what is necessary to cover all or part of the costs incurred in the discharge of the public service obligations, taking into account the relevant receipts and a reasonable profit.

4.   Where the undertaking is not chosen in a public procurement procedure, the level of compensation needed must be determined by a comparison with an analysis of the costs which a typical transport undertaking would incur.

Public compensation will not be state aid if these four conditions are met.

Aid must be Granted by Member State or from Member State Resources

[14.04] The provisions of Art 107 TFEU outline that aid must be granted by a Member State or from Member State resources. The court has held that this includes the resources of local and regional authorities. This was established in *Intermills* (Case 323/82), [1984] ECR 3809.

THE MEASURE MUST DISTORT OR THREATEN TO DISTORT COMPETITION

[14.05] In *Philip Morris Holland BV v Commission* (Case C–730/ 79), [1980] ECR I–2671 the court stated that when state aid strengthens the position of one undertaking but no other undertakings competing in intra-Community trade, competition is affected by that aid.

The General Court has provided further guidance in this matter in the case of *Confederacion Espanola de Transporte de Mercancias (CETM) v Commission* (Case T–55/99), [2000] ECR II–3207. In this case the General Court stated that where a Member State grants aid to an undertaking, internal market supply may be maintained or increased with the consequence that the opportunities for undertakings established in other Member States to offer their services to the market of that Member State are reduced.

The Commission enjoys a wide discretion in terms of Art 107(3) TFEU. If the Commission decides that the aid does not constitute aid within the meaning of Art 107 TFEU then the state aid prohibition rules do not apply. However, if the aid is deemed to be state aid within the meaning of Art 107 TFEU the Commission can find that the aid is compatible pursuant to Art 107(2) or 107(3) or it could make a finding of incompatibility with the internal market.

PROCEDURAL RULES ON STATE AID

[14.06] Articles 108 and 109 TFEU contain the procedural rules on the notification of state aid. The case law of the Court of Justice of the European Union has contributed to the interpretation of these provisions. In addition, Council Regulation (EC) 659/99 provides further clarification on the procedural rules. The applicable rules differ depending on whether the state aid is an existing state aid or whether it is a new state aid.

EXISTING STATE AID

[14.07] Article 108(1) TFEU states that:

> 'The Commission shall, in cooperation with Member States, keep under constant review all systems of aid existing in those States. It shall propose to the latter any appropriate measures required by the progressive development or by the functioning of the internal market'.

This means that the Commission had a duty to keep state aid under constant review and there is no requirement to notify the Commission of state aid. If the Commission forms the view that existing state aid is no longer compatible with the common market, the Member State must be informed and it must be given one month to submit its comments. On foot of the comments received from the Member State the Commission will decide whether or not the state aid is contrary to EU law. If the state aid is contrary to EU law the Commission can issue a recommendation proposing amendments or it can look for the abolition of the state aid.

The Commission can invoke Art 108(2) TFEU and use the formal investigation procedure when a Member State does not agree with its recommendation. A definition of existing state aid has been obtained from *Namur* (Case C–44/93) and *Gibraltar v Commission* (Case D–195/01).

In *Namur* the court held that when considering whether or not state aid is existing or new it is necessary to look at the legislative framework surrounding the state aid and it is not necessary to look at the amount of the state aid. The guidelines from the court were further supplemented by the procedural regulations and the following categories of state aid can be considered to be existing state aid:

1. Aid which existed before the entry into force of the Treaty;

2. Aid to which the Commission has granted an exemption under Article 107(3) TFEU;

3. Aid notified to the Commission which is not yet the subject of a decision;

4. Aid not recoverable because the limitation period has expired; and

5. Aid which was not state aid at the time it was made but became state aid as a result of the evolution of the common market.

NEW STATE AID

[14.08] Any state aid that is not classified as existing is termed as new state aid for the purpose of the Treaty provisions. If the state aid is classified as new it must be notified to the Commission before it can be granted. The Treaty provision on new state aid is contained in Art 108 TFEU. Article 108(3) TFEU outlines the first part of the procedural process.

'The Commission shall be informed in sufficient time to enable it to submit its comments of any plans to grant or alter aid. If it considers that any such plan is not compatible with the internal market having regard to Article 107 it shall without delay initiate the procedure provided for in paragraph 2. The Member State concerned shall not put its proposed measures into effect until this procedure has resulted in a final decision.'

Pursuant to these provisions, a Member State has an obligation to notify the Commission of any new state aid or proposed changes to existing state aid and the Commission must authorise new state aid. The Commission must consider the legality of the state aid within a two month timeframe. If the two-month timeframe expires the Commission is deemed to have authorised the aid and consequently a Member State can implement this state aid after giving prior notice to the Commission. The Commission can give a decision within fifteen days of receiving this notice from the Member State and this may result in the Member State being unable to implement the new state aid. At the end of the three months the Commission has three options available to it:

1. It can decide that the measure does not constitute state aid;

2. Pursuant to Art 107(2) TFEU, it can decide that the measure is compatible with the common market;

3. Pursuant to Art 108(2) TFEU, it will initiate a formal investigation as it suspects the aid is not compatible with the common market.

The second stage of the procedural process is contained in Article 108(2). It states the following:

'If after giving notice to the parties concerned to submit their comments the Commission finds that aid granted by a state or through state resources is not compatible with the internal market, having regard to Article 107 or that such aid is being misused, it shall decide that the state concerned shall abolish or alter such aid within a period of time to be determined by the Commission.

If the State concerned does not comply with the decision within the prescribed time the Commission or any other interested State may in derogation from the provisions of Article 258 and 259 refer the matter to the Court of Justice directly.'

[14.09] Therefore Art 108(2) TFEU applies to both existing state aid and new state aid. It will apply to existing state aid when the legality of the state aid is under review pursuant to Art 108(1) and it will apply to new state aid that comes under review at the preliminary notification stage.

According to Art 108(3) TFEU, a Member State is required to notify the Commission if they receive any aid exceeding €200,000 over three years and consequently there will be an assessment carried out to see if the aid is compatible with the internal market. Any aid below €200,000 is not seen as capable of affecting trade between Member States. Once a notification is received the Commission will then consider whether the aid falls within the Art 107 TFEU prohibition. The Commission will conduct the assessment pursuant to Art 107(2) TFEU provisions which outline when aid shall be compatible with the internal market.

Interested parties can submit comments once the Commission has published a notice in the official journal. The Member States and/or the Commission can have the matter sent directly to the Court of Justice of the European Union. The Commission has eighteen months within which to reach a final decision and the three results available to the Commission are:

1. the advantage is not state aid;

2. the advantage is compatible with the common market; or

3. the advantage is incompatible with the common market

RECOVERY OF UNLAWFUL STATE AID

[14.10] According to Article 108(3) and Council Regulation (EC) 659/99, the Commission can institute a formal investigation if it decides that the aid is not compatible with the internal market. A Member State can receive notice from the Commission to stop state aid within a designated timeframe, pursuant to Art 108(2). The Commission can recover any aid given to an undertaking which is incompatible with the provisions of a Treaty.

If a decision is made that state aid is contrary to EU law there is an obligation on the undertaking to repay the unlawful state aid. This can raise a number of problems for the undertaking concerned. However, the state aid must be repaid irrespective of any difficulties it may cause for the undertaking. In *Commission v Belgium* (Case C–52/84) the court stated that the only defence it would consider was that it was absolutely impossible for the state aid to be recovered. Therefore, submissions can only be made outlining the difficulties it will encounter if it has to repay the state aid.

THE BANKING CRISIS

[14.11] The provision of state aid has come under considerable scrutiny in recent years, particularly due to the banking crisis. As a result, the Commission has issued new guidelines to help national courts when they are applying state aid rules. There are also guidelines for national governments. The guidelines outline that aid is permitted when six basic conditions are met. To be permitted the state aid must:

1.   Give non-discriminatory access to the aid.

2.   The advantage must not be limited in time.

3.   The advantage must be limited in scope.

4.   An appropriate private-sector contribution should be sought.

5.   Behavioural rules to avoid abuse of the aid should be in place.

6.   A suitable follow-up structure should be put in place.

In recent years these conditions have been used extensively by the governments throughout Europe. In *CELF* (Case C–1/09), [2010] ECR I–2099 the Court of Justice outlined the procedure a national court should follow when unlawful state aid had to be recovered. The Court of Justice stated that it would not be appropriate for a national court to stay proceedings in this situation and that a ruling must be given, even if a decision was pending from the Commission. The court stated that if the national court did not give the decision it would be facilitating the continuation of an unfair advantage.

Chapter 15

Mergers

INTRODUCTION

[15.01] The TFEU does not outline or contain provisions on merger control. In the absence of Treaty provisions on merger control the case law on Arts 101 and 102 TFEU has been utilised and applied to mergers.

Mergers are currently regulated by Council Regulation (EC) 139/2004 which replaced Council Regulation (EEC) 4064/89. Council Regulation (EC) 139/2004 operates in conjunction with the Implementing Regulation 802/2004. Regulation 139/2004 contains the main rules for the assessment of mergers and the Implementing Regulation 802/2004, as amended by Council Regulations (EC) 1033/2008 and (EU) 1269/2013, contains the procedural information.

In Ireland merger control was governed by Pt 3 of the Competition Act 2002 and notifications for mergers coming within the Competition Act thresholds were made to the Competition Authority until the enactment of the Competition and Consumer Protection Act 2014. The Competition and Consumer Protection Act 2014 has made a number of significant changes to Irish merger control. One of the main changes is that the Competition Authority and the National Consumer Agency have now been amalgamated to form the Competition and Consumer Protection Commission.

MERGER REGULATION (EC) 139/2004

[15.02] It is accepted that undertakings will merge as part of common business practice however mergers that restrict competition are not allowed. Council Regulation (EC) 139/2004 on the control of concentrations between undertakings OJ 24/1, 29 January 2004 sets out the guidelines on appropriate merger control within the European Union.

Article 1 of Regulation (EC) 139/2004 states:

'1 Without prejudice to Article 4(5) and Article 22, this Regulation shall apply to all concentrations with the Community dimension as defined in this Article.

2 A concentration has a Community dimension where

(a)   the combined aggregate worldwide turnover of all the undertakings concerned is more than EUR 5000 million; and

(b)   the aggregate Community-wide turnover of each of the least two of the undertakings concerned is more than EUR 250 million,

unless each of the undertakings concerned achieves more than two-thirds of its aggregate Community-wide turnover within one and the same Member State.

3 A concentration that does not meet the thresholds laid down in paragraph 2 has a Community dimension where:

(a)   the combined aggregate worldwide turnover of all the undertakings concerned is more than EUR 2500 million;

(b)   in each of at least three Member States the combined aggregate turnover of all the undertakings concerned is more than EUR 100 million;

(c)   in each of at least three Member States included for the purpose of point (b), the aggregate turnover of each of at least two of the undertakings concerned is more than EUR 25 million; and

(d)   the aggregate Community-wide turnover of each of at least two of the undertakings concerned is more than EUR 100 million, unless each of the undertakings concerned achieves more than two-thirds of its aggregate Community-wide turnover within one and the same Member State.'

The various components of the regulation will now be considered in turn.

TYPES OF MERGERS

[15.03] Horizontal mergers are mergers between undertakings that produce the same products. Vertical mergers are mergers between undertakings that operate at different levels of the same product market.

CONCENTRATION

[15.04] The definition of concentration is contained in Art 3 of Regulation 139/2004. A concentration will occur where two previously independent undertakings merge and become one undertaking. Concentration is another word for merger. The term 'concentration' also relates to acquisitions and joint ventures.

A UNION DIMENSION

[15.05] Only concentrations that have a European Union dimension will be subject to the provisions of Council Regulation (EC) 139/2004. In order to have a Union dimension a concentration will have to meet certain thresholds of turnover as listed in the regulation.

THE ONE-STOP SHOP

[15.06] If a concentration meets the regulation thresholds it must notify the Commission and this prevents the filing of multiple cases in different Member States.

Exceptions to the One-Stop Shop Principle

[15.07]

- Article 4.4 of Council Regulation (EC) 139/2004 – referral from the authorities of a Member State on the application of the undertaking concerned;
- Article 4.5 of Council Regulation (EC) 139/2004 – referral from national authorities to the Commission on the application of the undertaking concerned;
- Article 9 of Council Regulation (EC) 139/2004 – referral from the Commission to the authorities of a Member State on the application of the Member State concerned;
- Article 22 of Council Regulation (EC) 139/2004 – referral from one or more Member States to the Commission.

NOTIFICATION OF CONCENTRATIONS UNDER REGULATION 139/2004

[15.08] Council Regulation (EC) 139/2004 requires the compulsory notification of any concentrations of undertakings with a European dimension.

The rule on notification is set out in Art 4(1) of Council Regulation (EC) 139/2004 and it states:

> 'Concentrations with a Community dimension defined in this Regulation should be notified to the Commission prior to their implementation and following the conclusion of the agreement, the announcement of the public bid, or the acquisition of a controlling interest.'

SIGNIFICANT IMPEDIMENT TO EFFECTIVE COMPETITION – THE SIEC TEST

[15.09] The test is set out in Art 2(3) of the Regulation and it states:

> 'A concentration which would not significantly impede effective competition in the common market or in a

substantial part of it, in particular as the result of the creation or strengthening of a dominant position, shall be declared compatible with the common market.

This is a broad test and it gives the Commission power to intervene in a concentration even if there is no dominant position.

THE COMMISSION GUIDELINES ON HORIZONTAL MERGERS

[15.10] In 2004, the Commission published guidelines on the assessment of horizontal mergers. The Guidelines outlined two ways in which horizontal mergers can significantly impede effective competition.

1. A horizontal merger can strengthen a dominant position through non-coordinated effects.

2. A horizontal merger can also strengthen a dominant position through coordinated effects.

TIME LIMITS

[15.11] Mergers are notified to the Commission using the Form CO and this is done electronically. Once the Commission has been notified the investigation must be completed within 25 days. This can be extended to 35 days. Once phase 1 is completed, the Commission gives a decision as to whether the proposed merger is compatible with the internal market. If it is compatible the matter is closed. If it is not compatible then a phase 2 assessment is commenced. The majority of cases do not need to go to a phase 2 investigation. In 2007, 402 cases were notified to the Commission, only 15 cases went onto phase 2 and from that 15 only one was prohibited. In 2007, the prohibited merger was *Ryanair/Aer Lingus* (Case COMP/M.4439).

In phase 2, the Commission has a 90-day time limit to rule as to whether or not the merger is compatible with the internal market.

The Court of Justice can intervene in order to give a decision on the legality of a Commission decision. Applications to consider the Commission's decision can only be made under Article 263 TFEU and this means that strict *locus standi* requirements apply.

THE MERGER SIMPLIFICATION PACKAGE

[15.12] The procedure for reviewing concentrations has been simplified by a package adopted by the European Commission. The Commission has reviewed its procedures through the Notice on simplified procedures and the merger implementing Regulation (EU) 1269/2013. The procedure widens the scope for unproblematic mergers and allows the simplified procedure to be applied to 60–70 per cent of cases. In addition, the total amount of information required in all notification cases whether simplified or not has been reduced. This will have a positive impact on reducing costs and preparatory notification work for businesses. The Merger Simplification Package came into effect on 1 January 2014.

IRISH MERGERS

[15.13] In Ireland mergers were previously governed by Pt 3 of the Competition Act 2002. When a merger satisfied the financial thresholds set out in the Act a notification had to be made to the Competition Authority. Section 18 of the 2002 Act required mandatory notification to the Competition Authority when the following was met:

- the worldwide turnover of each of two or more of the undertakings involved in the merger or acquisition is not less than €40m;

- two or more of any of the undertakings involved in the merger or acquisition carries on business in any part of the island of Ireland; and

- the turnover in the State of any one of the undertakings involved in the merger is not less than €40m.

The Competition and Consumer Protection Act 2014 amended the financial thresholds that require notification. The notification will now be made to the Competition and Consumer Protection Commission. The requirement that the undertakings involved have a turnover of €40m has been amended. The new thresholds are as follows:

- the aggregate turnover in the State of the undertakings involved is not less than €50m;

- the turnover in the State of each of two or more of the undertakings involved is not less than €3m.

The State in the new legislation refers to the Republic of Ireland.

It is a criminal offence not to notify the Competition and Consumer Protection Commission of a merger that meets the thresholds.

Where a merger has been notified to the Competition and Consumer Commission the Act provides for extended periods of review. For Phase 1, the timeframe for review is 30 working days and for Phase 2, it is 120 working days.

The Act also introduces a media merger regime that requires all media mergers to be notified to the Minister for Communications Energy and Natural Resources in addition to the Competition and Consumer Commission.

Irish Case Law on Mergers

[15.14] In *Ryanair Holdings plc and Aer Lingus Group plc v Commission* (Cases T–342/07 and T–411/07), the Court of Justice was called upon to consider the legality of the Commission's decision to refuse the merger between Aer Lingus and Ryanair. The General Court upheld the Commission's refusal to order Ryanair to divest its minority shareholding in Aer Lingus. The background to the case is that Aer Lingus was privatised by the Irish government in 2006 and Ryanair acquired a shareholding of 19.16 per cent in Aer Lingus at that time. Ryanair launched a public bid for the entire share capital of Aer Lingus on 23 October 2006 and notified the

Commission of its plan to take over in accordance with the merger regulation. The Commission gave a decision that Ryanair's planned takeover of Aer Lingus was incompatible with the common market. Ryanair brought an action against that decision in the Case T–342/07. Following the Commission's decision, Ryanair increased its shareholding in Aer Lingus to 29.3 per cent. Aer Lingus requested the Commission to make an Order outlining that Ryanair had to divest all of its shares in Aer Lingus. The Commission did not grant that request to Aer Lingus on the grounds that it was not within its power under the merger regulation. Aer Lingus then challenged that decision in Case T–411/07. Despite the challenge by both Ryanair and Aer Lingus, the General Court confirmed the two Commission decisions. Ryanair were unable to establish that the Commission was incorrect in its finding that a merger would significantly impede effective competition. In relation to Aer Lingus' challenge the General Court stated that the Commission had adhered to the legal standards required for merger control.

On 27 February 2013 the Commission prohibited the proposed takeover of Aer Lingus by Ryanair on the grounds of the EU Merger Regulation. The reason for the decision was that the merger would have resulted in harm to consumers as it would have combined the two leading Irish airlines resulting in a monopoly on 46 routes where Aer Lingus and Ryanair currently actively compete against each other. The merger would have reduced choice and inevitably led to price increases. Although Ryanair did offer remedies they were not sufficient and they did not satisfy the competition concerns raised by the Commission.

Chapter 16

Equality

INTRODUCTION

[16.01] Article 157 TFEU sets out the guidelines on equal pay and equal treatment. Article 157 TFEU states:

1. Each Member State shall ensure that the principle of equal pay for male and female workers for equal work or work of equal value is applied.

2. For the purpose of this article 'pay' means the ordinary basic or minimum wage or salary and any other consideration, whether in cash or in kind, which the worker receives directly or indirectly, in respect of his employment from his employer. Equal pay without discrimination based on sex means (a) that pay for the same work at piece rates shall be calculated on the basis of the same unit of measurement; (b) that pay for work at the time rates shall be the same for the same job.

3. The European Parliament and the Council, acting in accordance with the ordinary legislative procedure, and after consulting the Economic and Social Committee, shall adopt measures to ensure the application of the principle of equal opportunities and equal treatment of men and women in matters of employment and occupation, including the principle of equal pay for work of equal value.

4. With a view to ensuring full equality and practice between men and women in working life, the principle of equal treatment shall not prevent any Member State from maintaining or adopting measures providing for specific advantages in order to make it easier for the underrepresented sex to pursue a vocational activity or to

prevent or compensate for disadvantages in professional careers.

Directive 2006/54/EC consolidates the legislation in this area and provides clarification on Art 157 TFEU.

EQUAL PAY

[16.02] The Court of Justice has interpreted the term equal pay broadly and this broad definition of pay has led the court to consider whether or not pensions are pay within the meaning of Art 157 TFEU. In *Defrenne v Belgium* (Case C–80/70), [1971] ECR 445 the court considered if the definition of pay included state pensions. In this case a social security scheme funded a retirement pension through contributions from workers, employers and a state subsidiary. Defrenne argued that this pension constituted payment and as such was pay pursuant to Art 157 TFEU. The Court of Justice held that the definition of pay does not include state pensions.

Despite the ruling in *Defrenne* progress was made in the case of *Bilka Kaufhaus v Weber von Hartz* (Case C–170/84). *Bilka* concerned an occupational pension scheme and this scheme was funded completely by the claimant's employer. Due to this fact the Court of Justice held that the occupational pension scheme was pay for the purpose of Art 157 TFEU. The court stated the scheme and the rules governing it could be regarded as an integral part of the contract of employment between *Bilka* and its employees and benefits paid to employees under the scheme therefore constituted consideration received by the worker from the employer in respect of his employment as referred to in Art 157.

In *Barber v Guardian Royal Exchange* (Case C–262/88), a group of employees challenged their employer's pension scheme. Under the pension scheme men and women received their pensions at different ages. The court stated that social security benefits are not normally pay, however due to the fact that the pension scheme was funded by the employer this brought the pension scheme within the definition of equal pay.

BURDEN OF PROOF

[16.03] If an employee wants to bring an equal pay claim against their employer the employee must prove that his or her work is of equal value to another's work. However, if a pay system is complicated the burden of proof shifts and the employer must prove that there is no discrimination in the pay. This principle was established in *Handels-og Kontorfunktionaerernes Forbund i Danmark v Dansk (Acting for Danfoss),* (Case C–109/88). In *Danfoss* a claim was made that women were paid less than men. The Court of Justice held that the pay system lacked transparency and as a result this shifted the burden of proof to the employer.

DIRECT AND INDIRECT DISCRIMINATION

[16.04] Direct discrimination of grounds of pay is prohibited under Art 157 TFEU. This provision has been developed by the Court of Justice to include indirect discrimination. The court has stated that a direct discrimination cannot be justified. However, indirect discrimination can be justified by objective factors that do not relate to whether the employee is a man or a woman. The court provided a definition of these objective factors in the case of *Bilka Kaufhaus* (Case C–170/84). In *Bilka* an occupational pension scheme treated part-time employees differently to full-time employees. The court said that the difference in treatment was indirect discrimination. However, the court went on to say that such indirect discrimination could be justified in certain situations. The situations outlined by the court are as follows:

1. the company puts the measure in place in response to a real need such as an economic need;

2. the measure is appropriate;

3. the measure is necessary.

As a result of this test the court found that the discrimination could be objectively justified on economic grounds.

EQUAL TREATMENT

[16.05] The Treaty of Amsterdam introduced the concept of equal treatment. The equal treatment provisions are now contained in Directive 2006/54 and the provisions include promotion and work conditions. In *Marshall v Southampton and South West Area Health Authority* (Case C–152/84), [1986] ECR 723 the equal treatment directive was held to have direct effect.

This principle was developed further in the case of *Johnston v Chief Constable of the Royal Ulster Constabulary* (Case C–222/84). In this case the court held that the requirements of no discrimination in conditions of employment and no discrimination in regards to vocational training had direct effect. *Kreil* (Case C–285/98) concerned a German constitutional provision that excluded women from military posts where there was the use of arms. The applicant challenged this German law and the court held that the provision could not be justified as it went beyond the discretion afforded to Member States.

SOCIAL SECURITY DIRECTIVE 79/7/EEC

[16.06] The Social Security Directive extends the equal treatment provisions. The directive applies to statutory schemes that protect against sickness, invalidity, old age, accidents at work and occupational disease and unemployment (Art 3(1)). Article 2 states that the directive applies to all workers and self-employed persons whose activity is interrupted by illness, accident or involuntary unemployment and also person seeking employment. It also applies to retired or invalided workers and self-employed persons who are invalided. Article 4(1) of the directive states that direct and indirect sex discrimination including discrimination based on marital or family status is prohibited with respect to:

(1) the scope of social security schemes and access thereto;

(2) the obligation to contribute and calculation of contributions; and

(3) the calculation of benefits, including increases.

THE APPLICATION OF DIRECTIVE 79/7/EEC

[16.07] In the case of *Drake v Chief Adjudication Officer,* (Case 150/85), Mrs Drake had stopped working in order to care for her mother. She applied for an invalidity allowance, however she was denied it pursuant to national legislation. According to the national rules an invalidity allowance was payable to a married man but it was not payable to a married woman. The court held that Mrs Drake was entitled to the protection offered by the directive.

EXCEPTIONS TO THE PROHIBITION ON DISCRIMINATION

[16.08] Article 7 provides for an exception to the principles of non-discrimination that are provided for in Art 4 of the Directive. Article 7 states that the directive should be without prejudice to the right of Member States to exclude from its scope:

1. 'the determination of pensionable age for the purposes of granting old-age and retirement pensions and the possible consequences thereof for other benefits;

2. advantages in respect of old-age pension schemes granted to persons who brought up children, the acquisition of benefit entitlements following periods of interruption of employment due to the bringing up of children;

3. the granting of old-age or invalidity benefit entitlements by virtue of the derived entitlements of a wife;

4.   the granting of increases of long-term invalidity, old age, accidents at work and occupational disease benefits for a dependent wife;

5.   the consequences of the exercise, before the adoption of this Directive of a right of option not to acquire rights or incur obligations under a statutory scheme.'

These exceptions were tested in the case of *R v Secretary of State for Social Security* (Case C–9/91), [1992] ECR I–4297. This case concerned the Social Security Act 1975 in the UK. The Equal Opportunities Commission sought a declaration that the Social Security Act 1975 was in breach of Directive 79/7/EEC due to the fact that according to the provisions of the Act, the pensionable age for men was 65 and the pensionable age for women was 60. The Act also required men to make additional contributions towards their pension between the ages of 60 and 64.However, women were not required to make this contribution. The UK attempted to rely on the exception contained in Art 7 of the directive. The Court of Justice held that the discrimination was justified in order to maintain the financial equilibrium of a Member State's pension system.

Further clarification on the permitted forms of discrimination was provided in *Barber v Guardian Royal Exchange Assurance Group* (Case C–262/88). In this case Mr Barber challenged his employer's pension scheme due to the fact that it was payable at different ages for men and women. Mr Barber's employers had contracted out the pension scheme and the pension scheme in operation was actually in lieu of a statutory scheme. The court held that even though it was contracted out, the pension scheme did constitute pay within the meaning of Art 157 TFEU. As a result of this, the court also held that there must be equality with respect of the age at which the pension is received. If the pension is received at different ages, this means there is a difference of pay between men and women. The result of *Barber* was that Member States were required to bring statutory schemes and occupational schemes which were contracted out into line with each other.

EQUALITY AND PREGNANCY

[16.09] The case law from the Court of Justice has stated that if a woman is dismissed or refused employment due to the fact that she is pregnant, it is direct discrimination. The case law from the court has provided guidance on how this principle is to be interpreted.

In *Dekker v Stichting Vormingscentrum voor Jonge Volwassenen* (Case C–177/88) Mrs Dekker applied for the position of a training instructor at a youth training centre. When Mrs Dekker applied for the position she was pregnant and she informed her prospective employers of this fact. Mrs Dekker was chosen by the interview panel as being the most suitable candidate for the position. However, the youth training centre did not want to employ her because of the potential cost implications due to the fact that Mrs Dekker was pregnant when she applied for the job. The youth centre's insurance company would not pay any sickness benefit for Mrs Dekker's maternity leave. Mrs Dekker argued that the refusal to employ her was contrary to the Equal Treatment Directive 76/207/EEC and the court stated that as only women can be refused employment because of pregnancy, such refusal is direct discrimination. Due to this fact the Court of Justice found that the youth centre had acted in breach of the equal treatment directive and their actions could not be justified due to the financial losses they would suffer.

In *Brown v Rentokil Ltd* (Case C–394/96) the court stated that the principle of non-discrimination applied to both the length of the pregnancy and the length of maternity leave. As a result, any pregnancy-related illnesses that occurred before the birth and during the time of maternity leave could not be used as time periods for justifying dismissal.

In *Tele Danmark* (Case C–109/00), the employer offered a six-month fixed-term contract to work in their customer service department. When Tele Danmark offered the position the employee was already pregnant and consequently she knew she would be unable to see the six months of the contract to completion. Despite this fact she did not tell her employer that she was pregnant until she had completed one month of the contract. After informing her employer of the fact that she was pregnant she was dismissed. The case considered whether or not there was a duty to inform the employer of a pregnancy. The court held there is no duty to inform an employer of a pregnancy and a worker cannot be dismissed due to the fact that they were pregnant and they did not disclose this fact to the employer before commencing work. The issues relating to the position of pregnant women is now covered by the pregnancy directive, Directive 92/85/EEC, which covers matters such as working hours, leave, risk exposure and adjustment of working hours.

AGE DISCRIMINATION

[16.10] The court considered age discrimination in *Werner Mangold v Rudiger Helm* (Case C–144/04), [2005] ECR I–9981. In this case Mangold entered a fixed-term contract with the defendant when he was aged 56. The contract stated that due to the fact he was over 52 years of age when he commenced employment certain laws applied. The applicable German law lowered the age at which an employee could enter a fixed-term contract from 58 to 52. The German law permitted the employer to terminate the contract of employment without compensation if the employee was over the age of 52. Directive 2000/78/EC, the general framework directive on discrimination and employment was not in force at the time the application was brought by Mangold. Despite this fact Mangold attempted to argue that the German law was in contravention of the framework directive. The court concluded that if a piece of national law conflicted with the principle of equality generally, then the piece of national law must be set aside. The court confirmed its judgment in *Kucukdeveci* (Case C–555/07), [2010] ECR I–365. Ms Kucukdeveci was employed by a German company from when she was 18 years old. After ten years of employment she was dismissed by the company. However, she only received the notice period for an employee with three years' employment. The reason for this notice period was that a period of employment prior to the age of 25 could not be taken into account according to German legislation. The court reiterated its judgment in *Mangold* and stated that discrimination on grounds of age is prohibited.

The provisions of Directive 2000/78/EC were considered in the case of *Palacios de la Villa* (Case C–411/05), [2007] ECR I–8531 where the court outlined certain situations when Member States could provide for a difference in treatment on grounds of age. This case concerned an agreement that provided when a worker reached the age of 65 there would be an automatic termination of employment and an entitlement to a social security pension. The court held that in this situation discrimination could be justified.

The court went on to say that the Spanish legislation was adopted as part of a national policy aiming to promote better access to employment by means of better distribution of work between the generations. The fact that the legislation did not formally refer to an aim of that kind did not automatically exclude the possibility that it may be justified. The court considered that other elements, taken from the general context of the measure concerned, enabled its underlying aim to be identified for the purposes of judicial review as regards its justification.

Chapter 17

Fundamental Rights

INTRODUCTION

[17.01] The European Union primarily began as an economic union and the first EC Treaty did not contain provisions on fundamental rights. However, as the principles of EU law developed it became clear that fundamental rights required protection.

The Court of Justice of the European Union played a pivotal role in the development of fundamental rights protection. The court acknowledged that fundamental rights had to be recognised as a general principle of EU law. This was necessary in order to ensure that fundamental rights were adequately protected. In *Stauder v City of Ulm* (Case 29/69), [1969] ECR 419 the court implicitly recognised that fundamental rights had to be protected under EU law and by the court.

The court expanded on the *Stauder* ruling in *International Handelsgesellschaft GmbH* (Case 11/70), [1970] ECR 1125. In this case the court was asked to consider whether a deposit system under Council Regulation (EEC) 120/67 was contrary to German constitutional law. In relation to fundamental rights the court made the following observation,

> 'Respect for fundamental rights forms an integral part of the general principles of law protected by the Court of Justice. The protection of such rights, whilst inspired by the constitutional traditions common to the Member States, must be ensured within the framework of the structure and objectives of the Community'.

The court repeated the assertions in *Nold v Commission* (Case 4/73), [1974] ECR 1125 and stated that fundamental rights were envisaged and created by international treaties in order to ensure the protection of human rights and the Member States of the European Union had collaborated on these documents and treaties of which they were

179

signatories. However, the court went on to say that fundamental rights could be subject to limitations and these limitations could be justified by EU objectives.

[17.02] The Treaties now formally recognise the jurisprudence of the court and direct references are made to the protection of fundamental rights. Article 6(1) of Treaty on European Union (TEU), as amended by the Treaty of Amsterdam (ToA), provides that the Union is founded on principles of liberty, democracy, respect for human rights and fundamental freedoms and the rule of law. The ToA inserted a new Art 7 TEU which provided that Member States could have their voting and other rights suspended for breaches of fundamental rights.

However, despite these advances in *Re the Accession of the Community to the ECHR (Opinion 2/94)* [1996] ECR I–1759 it was stated that the EU did not have the necessary competence to accede to the European Convention on Human Rights (ECHR)

In 1999, the Council launched an initiative to create a Charter of Fundamental Rights. A Convention comprising of MEPs, national MPs and representatives from the Member States and the EU Commission was established to draft a document on fundamental freedoms for the European Union. The Convention drew up the Charter of Fundamental Rights of the European Union which was approved by the Member States at the Nice Summit in December 2000.

> The Charter was only declaratory and not legally binding. This position was changed by the Lisbon Treaty and fundamental rights provisions are now contained in Art 6 TEU, which provides as follows:
>
> '1. The Union recognises the rights, freedoms and principles set out in the Charter of Fundamental Rights of the European Union of 7 December 2000, as adapted at Strasbourg, on 12 December 2007, which shall have the same legal value as the Treaties.

The provisions of the Charter shall not extend in any way the competences of the Union as defined in the Treaties.

The rights, freedoms and principles in the Charter shall be interpreted in accordance with the general provisions in Title VII of the Charter governing its interpretation and application and with due regard to the explanations referred to in the Charter, that set out the sources of those provisions.

2. The Union shall accede to the European Convention for the Protection of Human Rights and Fundamental Freedoms. Such accession shall not affect the Union's competences as defined in the Treaties.

3. Fundamental rights, as guaranteed by the European Convention for the Protection of Human Rights and Fundamental Freedoms and as they result from the constitutional traditions common to the Member States, shall constitute general principles of the Union's law.'

Following the Lisbon Treaty coming into force, the Charter of Fundamental Rights has been elevated to the same status as the Treaties. However the Czech Republic, the United Kingdom and Poland have negotiated an opt-out of the Charter of Fundamental Rights. The EU can now accede to the ECHR and the fundamental rights guaranteed by the ECHR are general principles of EU Law. Accession is an act by which a state signifies its agreement to be legally bound by the terms of a particular treaty. Therefore, if the EU accedes to the European Convention on Human Rights it would become a party to the Convention. Since the European Convention on Human Rights is an independent international document which is not created by the European Union, the EU must accede to the ECHR if it decides to become a party to the Convention

THE CHARTER OF FUNDAMENTAL RIGHTS

[17.03] The Charter of Fundamental Rights contains six sections entitled:

1. Dignity

2. Freedoms

3. Equality

4. Solidarity

5. Citizens' Rights

6. Justice

The Charter of Fundamental Rights is now a legally binding document. Before this new status was achieved the court used the provisions of the Charter for guidance on the existence and identification of fundamental rights protected under EU law.

Prior to the Charter becoming a legally binding document the court made reference to the provisions of the Charter in its case law. In *European Parliament v Council* (Case C–540/03), [2006] ECR I–5799 the court stated approvingly that the principal aim of the Charter is to reaffirm rights as they result from the constitutional traditions and international obligations common to the Member States, the Treaty on European Union, the Community Treaties, the Social Charters adopted by the Community and by the Council of Europe and the case-law of the Court of Justice and of the European Court of Human Rights.

Article 51 of the Charter on Fundamental Rights states that:

> 'The provisions of this Charter are addressed to the institutions, bodies, offices and agencies of the Union with due regard for the principle of subsidiarity and to the Member States only when they are implementing Union law. They shall therefore respect the rights, observe the principles and promote the application thereof in accordance with their respective powers and respecting the limits of the powers of the Union as conferred on it in the Treaties.'

The Charter applies to the European institutions and Member States when they implement EU law.

THE EUROPEAN CONVENTION ON HUMAN RIGHTS

[17.04] The UN Declaration on Human Rights was adopted in 1948 following World War II and subsequently, the European Convention on Human Rights (ECHR) was drafted in 1949. The ECHR is an international agreement that protects human rights and fundamental freedoms. By signing the convention a country is pledging to honour its obligations under the provisions contained in the convention.

The European Convention on Human Rights is a piece of international law and Ireland signed the European Convention on Human Rights in 1955. Even though Ireland was a signatory to the Convention, the Convention did not become part of Irish law until it was incorporated by the European Convention on Human Rights Act 2003. Pursuant to the Irish Constitution international law does not become part of Irish national law unless it is incorporated by an act of the Oireachtas. This means that until a piece of international law is incorporated it cannot be relied upon in an Irish court.

The treatment of international law within a particular country depends on whether the state operates a dualist or monist system. A dualist state treats international law as being entirely separate from national law. A monist state does not view international law as being separate and treats both international and domestic law as being one and the same. A monist state does not need to incorporate international law while a dualist state must incorporate it.

Ireland is a dualist state and therefore, international law must be incorporated. The European Convention on Human Rights could not be relied upon in Irish Courts until it was incorporated in 2003, even though Ireland was a signatory to the Convention since 1955.

The European Union is an exception to the principle of dualism. The Irish constitutional provisions that apply to international law do not apply to the European Union and European Union Laws. The European Union is a legal order that operates independently of international law and in conjunction with the national laws of Member States.

THE ECHR AND THE CHARTER ON FUNDAMENTAL RIGHTS

[17.05] The European Court of Justice and the European Court of Human Rights are separate institutions and their relationship will now be examined for the purpose of clarification:

- The **European Court of Justice** protects and vindicates the rights contained in the Treaties of the European Union.

- The **European Court of Human Rights** protects and vindicates the rights contained in the European Convention on Human Rights (ECHR).

The fundamental rights protected by the Charter on Fundamental Rights include many rights which are also contained in the ECHR and its protocols. For example, Art 7 of the Charter protects the right to respect for private and family life and this resembles Art 8 of the ECHR. The Charter also protects the right to property which is also protected in Art 1 of Protocol 1 of the ECHR.

The developments established by the Lisbon Treaty create a variety of new questions and considerations in the area of fundamental rights protection. Currently there is an extended fundamental rights framework within the European Union, however the EU's accession to the ECHR is now questionable. Many commentators believe that accession is no longer desirable given that the EU now has a Charter on fundamental rights which is binding.

[17.06] However talks and negotiations on accession continue to take place between negotiators, representatives of the 47 Council of Europe Member States and the European Union. Together they have finalised a draft accession agreement of the European Union to the European Convention on Human Rights. The draft agreement outlines the scope of accession, how cases would operate and the participation required from the EU. An opinion from the Court of Justice is now required in order to outline the compatibility of the draft agreement with the EU Treaties.

The arguments in favour of accession to the ECHR are varied and diverse. Those in favour of accession argue that the EU is only focused on economic goals, the Court of Justice has too many political interests and the European Court for Human Rights (ECtHR) in Strasbourg has true expertise in the area of human rights.

[17.07] Despite the arguments in favour of accession there are some practical consequences of accession which must be considered. If accession does occur the Court of Justice will no longer decide on the lawfulness of EU action which is alleged to violate human rights. The European Court for Human Rights in Strasbourg would decide all these matters.

Currently the European Court for Human Rights will not admit complaints brought directly against the EU as it is not a party to the ECHR. However, the ECtHR has entertained indirect complaints against the EU which were brought against one or all of the Member States. This occurred in the case of *Bosphoros v Ireland (App no 45036/98)* (2006) 42 EHRR 1. The ECtHR concluded that once a Member State is acting in accordance with EU law it is absolved of any duties or responsibilities it has under the European Convention on Human Rights. The ECtHR relied on the fact that EU fundamental rights protection was equal to the protection provided by the ECHR.

The complex but co-operative relationship between the Court of Justice and the ECtHR is highlighted as negotiations continue on the accession of the European Union to the European Convention on Human Rights. The last meeting took place in April 2013 and the next steps are still forthcoming.

INDEX